Big Secrets

William Poundstone

BIG SECRETS

The Uncensored Truth About All Sorts of Stuff You Are Never Supposed to Know

QUILL

NEW YORK

The following recipes are used with permission of The AVI Publishing Company, Inc., 250 Post Road East, Westport, CT 06881: Cola Flavor Base (MF 238), Cola Flavor (MF 241), Benedictine-Type Cordial Flavor (MF 297), and Grand "M"-Type Flavor from pages 332–333, 333–334, 392–393, and 405, respectively, of *Food Flavorings* by Joseph Merory, 1968; Angostura Essence (MF 296A) and Italian Bitter Essence (MF 314A) from pages 806 and 817 of *Source Book of Flavors* by Henry B. Heath, 1981.

The recipe for Chartreuse flavor is reprinted with permission from page 625 of *Fenaroli's Handbook of Flavor Ingredients,* edited, translated, and revised by Thomas E. Furia and Nicolo Bellanca. Copyright © 1971 by CRC Press, Inc., Boca Raton, FL.

The outlines of the Rorschach blots are reproduced courtesy of Verlag Hans Huber, Bern, Switzerland.

The excerpts from *The Amazing World of Kreskin* by Kreskin are reprinted with permission of Random House, Inc. Copyright © 1973 by Kreskin.

The initiation stunts from *Initiation Stunts* by Lieutenant Beale Cormack are described by permission of the publisher, Baker's Plays, Boston. Copyright 1922 by Fitzgerald Publishing Corporation. Copyright in renewal 1950 by Walter Ben Hare.

Library of Congress Cataloging in Publication Data

Poundstone, William.
  Big secrets.

  Includes index.
  1. Trade secrets. I. Title.
HD38.7.P68   1985   031'.02   85-3603
ISBN 0-688-04830-7 (pbk.)

Printed in the United States of America

26 27 28 29 30

BOOK DESIGN BY VICTORIA HARTMAN

To Judith Schnerk

Preface

The subject matter of this book ought not to exist at all. This is a book about institutional secrets—big secrets, secrets that affect the masses. It may seem incredible that something like a club handshake or a franchised fried chicken recipe can remain a secret. Surely too many insiders know the secret (and might talk). Surely too many outsiders are exposed to the secret (and might surmise it). Yet, by and large, institutional secrets remain secrets.

No harm is done by most institutional secrets. But it is only natural to be curious about them. The best gossip, after all, is gossip somebody doesn't want you to hear. Would anyone other than a chemist care what is in Coca-Cola if the Coca-Cola Company were not so loath to discuss the ingredients? Would the reversed message in Pink Floyd's *The Wall* be as intriguing if you could play it on an ordinary stereo? Would you puzzle over Doug Henning's magic if not for his smug assurance that you really don't want to know how it is done? Here, then, is a whole book about what people don't want you to know.

Few secrets are imponderable mysteries. The knack of doing a book such as this is to find out whom to talk to. I have been aided by all those who suggested topics or lines of research, directed me to friends of friends, revealed secrets, and provided advice and assistance. Thanks to Benton Arnovitz, Nicholas Bakalar, James S. Bradbury, Michael Chellel, Karon Corley, the staff of the Cornell University libraries, Paul Crouch, Jr., Mitch Douglas, Norman Farnsworth, Charles P. Grier, Cynthia Hayes, Luis Herrero, E. J. Kahn, Jr., Valerie Battle Kienzle, Gerry Kroll, Stuart C. Lerner and the staff of Associated Analytical Laboratories, James Mastroberti, Russell D. Meltzer, Cheryl Messemer, Julia F. Morton, Ric Myers, Gloria and Paul Pitzer, George A. Pollak, Stefan Rudolf and the staff of High Rise Sound, Daniel Schindler, Beverly Smith, Stewart Stogel, Barry Streims, Theresa Sullivan, and Rosalie Muller Wright.

And thanks especially to those who asked that their names not be mentioned.

Contents

PART FOUR / Alice, Let's Cheat   115
Tests. Read carefully, you may be responsible for this
material.

PART FIVE / Pay No Attention to the Man Behind the Curtain   143
Magic and psychics. All you need to know to spoil it for
everyone else.

PART SIX / Always the Last to Know   181
Media. What we have here is a failure to communicate.

PART ONE

Going to Hell in a Shopping Basket

I t's really your parents' fault. But how were they supposed to know that the Gee-Whiz ElectroShock Toilet Trainer wasn't the latest scientific development? Now you've got the cleanest apartment in town and a five-dollar-a-day Bon Ami habit. You're on a first-name basis with *E. coli*. And you know it's a none-too-spic-'n'-span world out there, chock full of lax personal hygiene and shrimp somebody forgot to devein. Given the propensity of hairnets for finding their way into corn dogs, you probably like to know exactly what's in food before you eat it. Well, *tough*. The processed-food industry isn't a restaurant, and you'll have to take what everyone else is eating. Food is not enough; most people want mystery. Secret recipes, secret sauces, secret spices. Millions of hearty eaters like postindustrial *je ne sais quoi* and are willing to pay for it. If there's a life beyond Dr Pepper, it's as welcome at the Safeway as a wet cleanup in aisle nine. Mom was right: Don't play with your food; you never know where it's been.

But how can big companies keep their secret recipes secret from the hundreds of employees who prepare the stuff? They can't. As the following pages demonstrate, the corporate grapevines have plenty to say.

1·

Kentucky Fried Chicken

As far as anyone knows, Colonel Harland Sanders revealed his recipe for Kentucky Fried Chicken to just two living souls. One was his wife, Claudia. The other was Jack C. Massey, head of the three-man syndicate that purchased the Kentucky Fried Chicken Corporation from Sanders in 1964.

Apparently, none of the five thousand Kentucky Fried Chicken franchisees has ever been told the full recipe. New restaurant operators attend "KFC University," a company-owned outlet in Louisville. There they are initiated into the special cooking method. They aren't told what is in the seasoning mix, however. Franchisees must buy the seasonings premixed from the Kentucky Fried Chicken Corporation. Some outlets buy ten-ounce packets of seasonings that are to be mixed with twenty-five pounds of flour. Others buy a preseasoned coating mix that contains the flour.

No Platinum in There

Ever since the Kentucky Fried Chicken chain mushroomed in the mid-1960s, the secret recipe has been the object of speculation. Examination of the chicken shows that the coating is a thin, almost soggy layer (in the "original recipe"; there is also a "spicy-crispy" version) adhering to the skin. The meat is notably moist, allegedly because of the special pressure-cooking process. There is little popular conviction as to what seasonings figure in the "secret blend of eleven herbs and spices." The chicken is flavorful,

| 13

but no herb or spice predominates. *The New York Times* quoted Sanders as maintaining that the herbs and spices "stand on everybody's shelf."

The presumption that the seasonings in Kentucky Fried Chicken are in fact perfectly ordinary ones has long been a bone of contention between franchisees and Kentucky Fried Chicken management. Restaurateurs are charged a steep price for the seasonings—more than any conceivable combination of herbs and spices ought to cost, say franchisees. In a 1976 book on McDonald's (*Big Mac: The Unauthorized Story of McDonald's* by Max Boas and Steven Chain), McDonald's founder Ray Kroc observed: "Kentucky Fried Chicken licensees claimed that they were paying three to four to five times for the same herbs and for the same chicken, and that they could get it from Durkee's or Kraft or any big company in the United States. And Kentucky Fried Chicken said, no, you couldn't because the formula was a secret. You know that was a lot of crap. Any laboratory can tell you what's in it. There's no platinum in there. There's no gold in there."

That there isn't platinum or eye of passenger pigeon in the mix is supported by the fact that the colonel occasionally whipped up the seasoning mixture impromptu. In Sanders' autobiography, *Life as I Have Known It Has Been Finger Lickin' Good,* he tells of selling his first franchisee, Leon "Pete" Harmon, on the chicken. Sanders concocted a batch of the seasoning mix from the pantry of Harmon's Salt Lake City restaurant.

Granting that all of the colonel's seasonings could be found at any well-stocked A&P, the task of identifying them remains formidable. There are approximately forty herbs, spices, and other seasonings available in American supermarkets and gourmet stores. Of these, perhaps twenty or thirty are common enough to "stand on everybody's shelf," figuratively speaking, and to have been in use at Sanders' roadside cafe. The use of eleven different seasonings is not remarkable. The standard "poultry seasoning" of the food industry has ten herbs and spices: pepper, ginger, mace, allspice, cloves, marjoram, nutmeg, thyme, savory, and sage.

In 1974 *Esquire* magazine asked four food writers to try Kentucky Fried Chicken and offer their analyses. There was little consensus.

James Beard found the chicken "well seasoned with salt"; with less assurance, he thought he detected monosodium glutamate, cayenne pepper, and cinnamon. Roy Andries de Groot was "reasonably sure of minuscule amounts" of rosemary, savory, tarragon, thyme, pepper, turmeric, and cinnamon. He also noted salt, monosodium glutamate, "tiny globules of what might be honey or brown sugar," and "the faintest touch of both almond and mint." Waverly Root concluded that the chicken was "dunked in some sort of batter" containing flour, milk, and perhaps egg. Root was certain only of salt and pepper in the seasoning; he guessed that celery salt, caraway, chili powder, and/or horseradish might be present. James Villas doubted that any milk or egg was used in the coating and further doubted that there were eleven herbs and spices. He detected only cinnamon and cloves. Villas argued that the secret of Kentucky Fried Chicken is sugar: "Real fried chicken is not sweet; this is." The sugar, he suspected, was added to the "very light and very safe and very healthy cooking oil."

Another analysis comes from Gloria Pitzer, a St. Clair, Michigan, homemaker and newsletter publisher. Pitzer's *Secret Recipe Report* attempts to duplicate the recipes of popular processed foods for home use. In the late 1970s, Pitzer devised three recipes for facsimile Kentucky Fried Chicken.

The recipes call for the chicken pieces to be fried in a pan or deep fryer until brown and then transferred to an oven for thirty to thirty-five minutes' additional cooking. One-fourth to one-half inch of water in the baking pan keeps the chicken moist in the oven. In Pitzer's first recipe, the chicken is seasoned with a marinade made from commercial Italian salad dressing mix, flour, salt, lemon juice, and oil.

Pitzer's second and third recipes use eleven herbs and spices each. The second, said to simulate spicy-crispy Kentucky Fried Chicken, requires garlic salt, onion powder, paprika, black pepper, allspice, sweet basil, oregano, sage, summer savory (substitution: parsley flakes), ginger, and rosemary. All are mixed with flour and salt. Chicken pieces are dampened with beer or club soda, dredged in the flour/seasoning mix, and fried.

The third recipe uses a modified list of herbs and spices: rosemary, oregano, sage, ginger, marjoram, thyme, parsley, pepper, paprika, garlic salt, and onion salt. Three additional flavorings— brown sugar, powdered chicken bouillon, and Lipton Tomato Cup-a-Soup mix—supplement the herbs and spices. Pitzer's recipes are the result of her own experimentation; she disavows any special knowledge of Kentucky Fried Chicken's actual recipe.

Does Phyllis George Know the Colonel's Recipe?

As late as June 1967, *Business Week* magazine could claim that "only Sanders, Massey [then chairman of the board of the corporation], and the company's food engineer know the recipe." This was not strictly correct. Sanders' wife, Claudia, certainly knew the recipe. It may be conjectured that other spouses, children, and business associates were told too.

Who Told Whom?
The Kentucky Fried Chicken Recipe

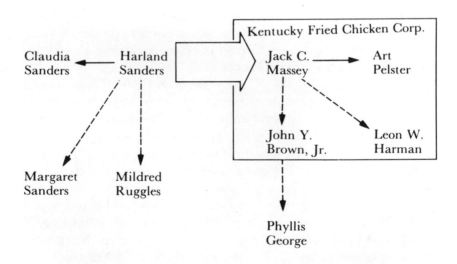

Claudia Sanders was a former employee at the Sanders Café in Corbin, Kentucky. In 1948 she became Sanders' second wife. Interstate 75 diverted the tourist traffic from the Sanders' motel/restaurant operation, forcing them to sell. The colonel took to the road at age sixty-six to promote his chicken franchise business. He had twenty-five white suits, always traveled with a pressure cooker and a bag of seasonings in the back seat of his Packard, and ate his chicken three to five times a week. Claudia stayed at home, mixed the secret seasonings, and sent them to franchisees. The colonel sold the business—too soon, too cheaply—in 1964, retaining the Canadian operation. He spent his last years praising the Lord and cursing the Heublein Corporation, which purchased the business from Sanders' buyers. Harland Sanders died in 1980 at the age of ninety. Claudia is proprietor of Claudia Sanders' Dinner House in Shelbyville, Kentucky.

It is hard to believe that the children weren't let in on the secret recipe. Sanders had two, both by his first marriage. At least one, Margaret, played a crucial role in the business by coming up with the idea of take-out service. For this Sanders gave her the franchise to the state of Florida. Margaret Sanders now lives in Palm Springs; sister Mildred Ruggles lives in Lexington, Kentucky.

The secret passed out of the family in 1964, when Sanders sold Kentucky Fried Chicken to a three-man syndicate for $2 million. Heading the syndicate was Jack C. Massey, a Nashville financier who had become bored with early retirement in Florida. Massey knew the secret, and so did food engineer Art Pelster. Pelster, originally an aerospace engineer, was in charge of mixing up the seasonings and refining the cooking method. He invented and patented several new types of frying and heating equipment for Kentucky Fried Chicken. Seven years after Massey's group bought the company, it was sold to Heublein, Inc.—purveyors of Smirnoff vodka, A.1 steak sauce, Snap-E-Tom tomato cocktail, Beaulieu Vineyard wines, Ortega Mexican food, and Arrow liqueurs—for a reported $287 million.

It is uncertain if Massey's two partners knew the recipe. One, Utah franchisee Leon "Pete" Harmon, seems to have had little role in day-to-day management. The other partner was attorney John Y. Brown, Jr. Brown helped convince Sanders to sell. After the sale, Massey groomed Brown to succeed him, and it seems a reasonable conjecture that Massey told Brown the secret recipe. Brown replaced Massey as chief executive officer and served as chairman of the board after the Heublein acquisition. (Massey left the company, reportedly after a tiff with Brown.) Profits from the sale to Heublein helped finance Brown's late, successful entry in the 1979 Kentucky gubernatorial race. Young, bright, and skillful at answering charges that he swindled an old man out of a chicken business, Brown is said to have higher political ambitions. ("Hell, governing Kentucky is easier than running Kentucky Fried Chicken," he told the press. "There's no competition.")

So the chain of initiates grew. If Brown knows the secret recipe, wouldn't he have told his wife, Phyllis George? Perhaps. A much-touted secret recipe might be more interesting to spouses, relatives, and friends than the average trade secret. A dozen or more people may now know the secret recipe, many of them not directly connected with the Kentucky Fried Chicken Corporation.

If so, they've been circumspect. No one has come forward to reveal the secret recipe.

Laboratory Analysis

Big Secrets selected a large college near a Kentucky Fried Chicken outlet. Advertisements asking that Kentucky Fried Chicken employees respond were placed in a student newspaper and on campus bulletin boards. Interviews with respondents revealed how the chicken is prepared. In essence, the descriptions agreed with Sanders' 1966 patent for a "process of producing fried chicken under pressure" (no. 3,245,800; copies available from the U.S. Patent Office).

The patent, of course, does not tell what seasonings are used. None of the respondents to the ads knew what seasonings are in the coating mix. Nor had they heard any rumors. But one respondent supplied a sample of the coating mix: a pungent-smelling white powder with black and tan flecks.

On the basis of Kroc's contention that any laboratory could tell what's in the mix, a food laboratory was consulted. It refused to do an analysis after hearing where the sample had come from. A second laboratory agreed to do an analysis. Approximately one cup of coating mix was sent for testing. The laboratory was asked to do a qualitative analysis—to identify everything in the sample, but not to worry about determining exact proportions. A list of likely herbs and spices compiled from Pitzer's recipes, the *Esquire* article, and the ingredients of the standard poultry seasoning was supplied as a starting point.

Based on the interviews, Sanders' patent, and the lab results, the secret recipe goes roughly like this:

Chickens weighing between 2¼ and 2½ pounds are preferred. They are cut into eight to ten pieces. What makes the Kentucky Fried Chicken recipe different from most others is that the quantity of chicken must be geared to the amount and temperature of the oil. If you try cooking just one piece of chicken in the usual amount of oil at the usual temperature, you get a cinder. This is why Sanders' method has not been duplicated widely at home.

For the typical five-pound batch cited in the patent, about eight quarts of oil at 400° F is needed. Sanders reasons in the patent description as follows: Chicken cooked by ordinary means tends to lose its natural moisture before the meat is fully done. Chicken tends to be undercooked or dried out. The obvious remedy is to cook the chicken in a watery liquid. Then the chicken looks and tastes "boiled." Furthermore, if a browned coating is desired, it often requires higher temperatures or longer cooking times than is appropriate for the chicken proper.

Sanders' solution is to start the cooking process at about 400° F—a high temperature that quickly browns the coating. A pressure cooker supplied with an air hose and pump is used. Continued cooking at 400° would incinerate the chicken, but the cold chicken and the generation of steam from the moisture in the coating lower the temperature of the cooking fat to about 250° F in a minute or two. The heating elements are then turned down to maintain a 250° F temperature throughout the remainder of the cooking cycle.

Meanwhile, the moisture boiling out of the chicken builds up the pressure in the closed vessel. If the various quantities have been measured correctly, a pressure of about fifteen pounds per square inch (above atmospheric pressure) is created. This raises the boiling point of water, and thus the actual cooking temperature of the moist chicken meat, to about 250° F. Under these conditions, chicken cooks two to ten times faster than in conventional cooking. The steam pressure prevents any further loss of moisture. If for some reason the steam pressure is not quite fifteen pounds per square inch, the air pump attached to the cooker makes up the difference. The total cooking time, including the browning phase, is about ten minutes. Then the pressure is released and the chicken is drained and stored in a warming oven (at about 160° F) until purchase.

There is no batter as such. The chicken pieces are "immersed in a dip made of skimmed or reconstituted skimmed milk and whole eggs (approximately eight per gallon of milk)," explains Sanders in his patent. "The dipped pieces are then rolled in flour to which has been added salt and other seasoning ingredients" and fried.

The seasonings, the most carefully guarded part of the Kentucky Fried Chicken recipe, yielded a surprise. The sample of coating mix was found to contain four and only four ingredients: flour, salt, monosodium glutamate, and black pepper. There were no eleven herbs and spices—no herbs at all, in fact. There was no sugar.

All the common herbs and spices can be identified unequivocally by trained personnel. Had there been so much as a good-sized grain or two of basil or nutmeg anywhere in the cup's worth of mix tested, it should have been detected, according to the director of the laboratory. Nothing was found in the sample that couldn't be identified.

The Kentucky Fried Chicken employees interviewed denied that anything was added to the chicken at any other stage in the cooking process—the seasonings in the coating mix are the only seasonings. This agrees with Sanders' own description of the cooking process in his patent. If the sample of coating mix tested was representative (and the company prides itself on the uniformity of its product), there seems to be no escaping the conclusion that there are no eleven herbs and spices. The real secret of Kentucky Fried Chicken, it seems, is simple and aimed dead center at the American palate: pepper and MSG.

Who's Killing the Herbs and Spices of Kentucky Fried Chicken?

It is possible that someone throws a pinch of each of the "missing" herbs and spices into the company seasoning vat every now and then. But if so, it seems that not a grain of anything other than pepper and MSG found its way into the sample tested, nor would it have found its way into any chicken made from the sample. (The sample should have been enough to coat a dozen or more pieces.) It seems presumptuous to claim eleven herbs and spices if the average piece of chicken does not contain a trace of each.

Maybe the colonel's original recipe had an honest eleven herbs and spices and the recipe was changed after he sold the company. There is certainly precedent for such tinkering. Prior to 1964, the

Kentucky Fried Chicken: An Ingredients List

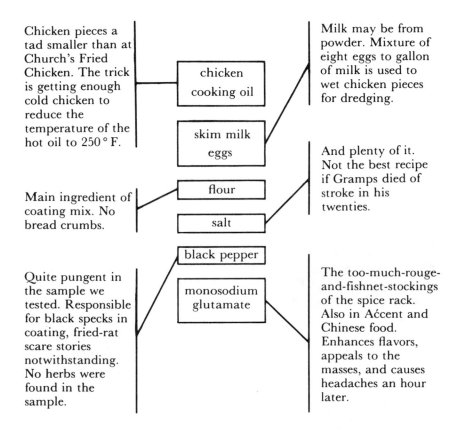

Chicken pieces a tad smaller than at Church's Fried Chicken. The trick is getting enough cold chicken to reduce the temperature of the hot oil to 250° F.

chicken
cooking oil

skim milk
eggs

flour

salt

black pepper

monosodium glutamate

Milk may be from powder. Mixture of eight eggs to gallon of milk is used to wet chicken pieces for dredging.

Main ingredient of coating mix. No bread crumbs.

And plenty of it. Not the best recipe if Gramps died of stroke in his twenties.

Quite pungent in the sample we tested. Responsible for black specks in coating, fried-rat scare stories notwithstanding. No herbs were found in the sample.

The too-much-rouge-and-fishnet-stockings of the spice rack. Also in Accent and Chinese food. Enhances flavors, appeals to the masses, and causes headaches an hour later.

Kentucky Fried Chicken gravy was pure ambrosia—"so good you can throw the chicken away and eat the gravy," boasted the colonel. But the new owners decided the gravy recipe was too labor-intensive for a fast-food operation and changed it. The result, charged Sanders, was "wallpaper paste." Kentucky Fried Chicken gravy remains a mediocre product, while the colonel's gravy recipe is presumably locked away, unused, in a company vault.

In all fairness, a chicken recipe with eleven seasonings probably has deadwood. If there was much pepper and MSG in the original recipe, they may have drowned out any subtler seasonings anyway.

2.

Food Horror Stories

Sex on Ritz Crackers

Little does Aunt Dagmar, who even clipped the recipe for Mock Apple Pie ("No Apples Needed"), suspect this scurrilous tale of prefab gastronomy. The word "SEX" is somehow baked onto the surface of Nabisco's Ritz Crackers—or so the story goes. The SEXes were "discovered" by subliminal advertising guru Wilson Bryan Key and first described in his 1976 book, *Media Sexploitation.* The SEXes are supposed to be scrawled in the irregular surface mottling of the crackers. Key finds about a dozen SEXes (in all-capital letters) on both the top and bottom surfaces. He suggests taking several crackers, placing them face up, and gazing at them for a few seconds. Provided you are relaxed, the secret SEXes are supposed to be visible. Key thinks the SEXes are created by special molds and that they are there to be perceived subliminally and thus to link subconsciously the eating of Ritz Crackers with sex. A lot of people think Key is nuts.

Is the Big Mac Secret Sauce
Just Thousand Island Dressing?

A few definitions are in order. To the processed-food biz, French dressing is a thin, pourable mayonnaise with a little tomato paste thrown in for color. Add chopped pickle to French dressing, and you have Thousand Island dressing. Add chopped bell pepper instead, and you have a bland incarnation of Russian dressing.

The Big Mac Secret Sauce plainly has a mayonnaise-type base. That is to say, it probably contains vegetable oil, water, vinegar, and egg yolk. Most mayonnaise also contains sugar. The Secret Sauce is the color of French dressing, but it contains chopped solids. If you scoop up a glob of the Secret Sauce and wash off the mayonnaise part, what is left? It seems to be chopped pickle, recognizable by the thin green skins adhering to white interiors. McDonald's may claim the exact composition of the sauce to be a secret, but it appears to be well within the conventional definition of Thousand Island dressing. In fact, the color of the Secret Sauce is a dead ringer for Kraft Thousand Island Dressing. For what it's worth, Kraft's list of ingredients reads: "Soybean oil, water, sugar, tomato paste, chopped pickle, vinegar, egg yolk, salt, mustard, flour, propylene glycol alginate, dehydrated onion, spice, calcium disodium EDTA to protect flavor, natural flavor."

According to McDonald's employees, corporate policy dictates exactly where the sauce is glopped onto the sandwich. There are thirteen layers in a Big Mac, two of them being dollops of Secret Sauce. The stacking order runs as follows: top bun, onions, meat, pickles, lettuce, Secret Sauce, middle bun, onions, meat, cheese, lettuce, Secret Sauce, bottom bun.

Sugar on Burger King French Fries

There may be no ice cream in fast-food "shakes," but there is sugar on the french fries. In an interview, Burger King president Donald Smith said that his chain's fries are sprayed with a sugar solution shortly before being packaged and shipped to individual outlets. The sugar carmelizes in the cooking fat, producing the golden color customers expect. Without it, the fries would be nearly the same color outside as inside: pasty white. Smith believes that McDonald's also sugar-coats its fries.

Is There Eggshell in Orange Julius?

It has been rumored that the secret behind this frothy mall fare is whole eggs—shells and all. Orange Julius is made by mixing orange juice with a mysterious white powder supplied by the company headquarters in Santa Monica, California. Thus the average Orange Julius employee has little idea what is in the drink.

If there are eggshells in the drink, they would have to be a component of that white powder.

The drink has an egglike smell. A recipe for a simulated "Orange Julius" has long been circulating. It calls for eight ounces of orange juice, one tablespoon of sugar syrup (mix sugar with just enough boiling water to dissolve), an egg, and about half a cup of crushed ice. All ingredients are mixed in a blender. Some people use the fluid part of the egg only; others throw the shell in too.

No bits of eggshell are apparent in a real Orange Julius. *Big Secrets* tried the above recipe, with the eggshells, to see if the shell fragments could be pulverized into invisibility. A whole, unbroken egg was plopped into eight ounces of orange juice, some syrup, and crushed ice in an Osterizer Galaxie blender. The blender was set on "Liquefy," the highest setting. After five minutes—far longer than the mixture would normally be blended—the liquid was poured out to check for shell fragments. The shell was still visible as a fine powder settled on the bottom of the blending chamber.

A letter asking about the eggshell story was sent to Orange Julius' headquarters. Orange Julius' reply: "There are no eggshells in an Orange Julius unless specifically requested by the customer."

Regular vs. Dry-Roasted Peanuts

Are dry-roasted peanuts less fattening? Just look at the labels. Vendors have managed to sell the idea of dry-roasted nuts as a diet aid, but they can't lie outright on the packages. Planter's Cocktail Peanuts have 170 calories an ounce. Planter's Dry-Roasted have 160 calories—scarcely enough of a difference to bother with. You do even worse with Planter's Salt-Free Dry-Roasted Peanuts, which contain not a calorie less per ounce (170) than the regular peanuts.

Two-Year-Old Fish in Worcestershire Sauce

Lea & Perrins' secret formula for Worcestershire sauce has been imitated widely. The label lists "water, vinegar, molasses, sugar, anchovies, tamarinds, hydrolyzed soy protein, onions, salt, garlic, eschalots, spices & flavorings" as ingredients—the only mystery being the "spices and flavorings."

Some conjecture that there must be dissolved anchovy bones in Worcestershire sauce. Whole anchovies go into the sauce; the sauce digests the fish as it ages. *People* magazine described the process in a 1982 profile of Worcestershire sauce heir Ransom Duncan: "Worcestershire [sauce] in various stages of aging sits in 35 6,000-gallon fir vats (which impart no flavor). 'That's been there quite a while,' notes Duncan, peering into a lumpy brown liquid. 'You can see onions, and you can see garlic. By this time you won't find fish; you might find skeletons. The meat begins to fall off and get absorbed.' "

The skeletons probably meet the same fate. Chicken bones dissolve in vinegar after a few weeks; Lea & Perrins' sauce is aged for a total of two years. Most of the water content is not added until shortly before bottling, so the liquid is largely vinegar.

The layer of crud at the bottom of a bottle of Worcestershire sauce has inspired its own speculation. The usual explanation is that it consists of tiny grains of the spices used. According to various standard recipes for Worcestershire sauce, common flavorings are Cayenne and black pepper, allspice, coriander, cloves, mace, crushed pickled walnuts, mushrooms, brandy, and sherry. The salient spice of Worcestershire sauce is something called asafetida or devil's dung—which may explain why it is never mentioned on the label.

Asafetida has a fetid odor and a bitter garlic/onion taste. It comes from a six-foot-tall carrotlike plant of Asia. When the top of the "carrot" is cut, a gummy resin—the asafetida—oozes out and dries as "tears" an inch across. At first a translucent pale yellow, the tears turn purple-streaked pink as they dry. Fully cured tears are opaque reddish-brown outside, milky-white inside. In the pure state, asafetida is used as a laxative; in Worcestershire sauce, a little goes a long way. According to a 1965 article in the *Journal of Food Technology,* the asafetida content of condiments runs from 5 to 160 parts per million.

Some Worcestershire sauces contain meat. Boiled pork liver is most frequently cited as an ingredient (some recipes demand it be cooked for eight to ten hours). Some recipes use beef extract.

None of the familiar commercial Worcestershire sauces list pork or beef on their labels. All, however, admit unspecified spices and flavorings. Pork is not a spice, but it could be a flavoring. French's, Crosse and Blackwell, and Ann Page Worcestershire sauces display the circled-U parve symbol. Parve food may contain fish (the anchovies), but it must not contain the meat of any mammal. Lea & Perrins and Heinz Worcestershire sauces do not have the parve symbol.

Big Secrets wrote the major Worcestershire sauce producers, asking if there is pork in their products. Lea & Perrins and French's denied any pork. Heinz and Crosse and Blackwell did not respond. But if Crosse and Blackwell is truly parve, it cannot contain pork. That leaves only Heinz as a possible pork-formula sauce.

What keeps the anchovies—and maybe pork—from spoiling without refrigeration? The vinegar and sugar keep them embalmed.

Stag's Leap vs. Stags' Leap

Every pop oenologist has heard of Stag's Leap, the Napa Valley *Wunderkind* that beat out several first growths of Bordeaux at a 1976 blind tasting in Paris. But before you shell out for a bottle, watch that apostrophe. Not to be confused with Stag's Leap Wine Cellars is Stags' Leap Winery, also of Napa Valley. A vinous knock-off? Not exactly. Each winery disputes the other's right to the name. Of course, only Stag's Leap won the Paris tasting. Restaurant wine lists are not above capitalizing on the confusion—and price differential.

Are Pink Peppercorns a Fraud?

Despite a thumbs-down from the Food and Drug Administration, hard-core *nouvelle cuisine* buffs still pay five to ten dollars an ounce for pink peppercorns. That's about what garden-variety caviar fetches; about ten times the cost of wild rice. Pink peppercorns are scarlet, about the size of regular peppercorns, and impart a bitter-pungent flavor to meat and fish. And pink peppercorns are slightly poisonous. They are suspected of causing headaches, chest congestion, nausea, intestinal inflammation, and hemorrhoids.

The extravagant price has always been justified by the source—the far-off isle of Réunion in the Indian Ocean. Pink peppercorns are harvested in Réunion by French firms, shipped to the mother country for processing, and then imported to the United States. They are sold in bulk, freeze-dried, or bottled in brine or vinegar.

Black pepper is the fruit of a vine. White pepper is black pepper with the skins removed. Pink peppercorns, however, are the fruit of an unrelated tree, *Schinus terebinthifolius*. *Schinus* is related to poison ivy, which explains its toxic potential.

Schinus is not found in Réunion only. The pink peppercorn tree is native to Brazil. It was introduced to Réunion long ago and has run wild there. *S. terebinthifolius* was also introduced into the southern half of Florida. There it goes by the names "Brazilian Pepper Tree" and "Florida Holly." It was brought to Florida as a sort of tropical holly for homesick transplants. During the Christmas season it fruits heavily, the boughs and red berries sometimes being used for Christmas decorations. *S. terebinthifolius* grows so rapidly in Florida that it has become a weed. Dotting roadsides, the tree and its berries are considered worse than useless. By one estimate, the tree now covers several thousand acres in Florida.

No one seems to have gotten the idea of selling the berries as pink peppercorns. A very similar tree, also with red berries, grows in Southern California (*Schinus molle*). The same *S. terebinthifolius* also grows in Hawaii. Anyone who orders salmon with *trois*-color peppercorns is paying over a hundred dollars a pound for a Fort Lauderdale weed.

3·

Coca-Cola

It is claimed that only two persons know the complete formula for Coca-Cola syrup. Company policy forbids them from traveling in the same plane. When one dies, the other is to choose a successor and impart the secret to that person. So secret is Coca-Cola's formula that the identity of the two initiates is itself a secret. Coca-Cola chairman Roberto Goizueta—a likely candidate because his background is in research and quality control—refused comment when *Fortune* magazine asked him in 1981 if he knew the formula. The written recipe is in a safe-deposit vault at the Trust Company of Georgia. The vault, it's claimed, can be opened only with the approval of the Coca-Cola board of directors. Clearly, the syrup recipe is perceived as the heart and soul of the Coca-Cola organization. Said the 1981 Coca-Cola annual report, commenting on the Columbia Pictures acquisition, "Programming is to the communications and entertainment businesses what syrup is to the beverage business."

Does Pepsi Know Coke's Secret?

Security was not always so tight. Coke's inventor, Atlanta pharmacist John Styth Pemberton, seems to have taken a casual attitude toward the recipe's secrecy.

In 1885 Pemberton mixed up a pirated version of a popular drink of the time, Vin Mariani. Vin Mariani was a wine spiked with coca leaves. It was both an aperitif and a stimulant—something on the order of Dubonnet, only with cocaine in it. According to a promotional book, Ulysses S. Grant, Jules Verne, Emile

Zola, Henrik Ibsen, the Russian Czar, and Pope Leo XIII drank Vin Mariani. (Some historians think it was responsible for Thomas Edison's insomnia.) Pemberton called his drink French Wine of Coca. Sales were disappointing.

The following year, Pemberton overhauled the formula. The wine was taken out. Still envisioning a stimulant product, he retained the coca leaf extract and added an extract of the African "hell seed" or kola nut. Kola nut contains caffeine, the same stimulant in coffee and tea.

Both coca and kola extracts are bitter. So Pemberton added sugar and flavorings to kill the unpleasant taste. The result was a syrup, not a beverage. The name "Coca-Cola" was adopted when Pemberton's partner, Frank M. Robinson, decided that two Cs would work well in the Spencerian-script logo he was designing.

During its first years in Atlanta, Coca-Cola was sold at pharmacies as a syrup that could be taken as is or diluted with water. Nothing on the market today is a counterpart of the early Coca-Cola. Coca-Cola was promoted as a stimulant—more the 1880s equivalent of No-Doz or Vivarin than just a drink. But No-Doz and Vivarin are not seen as particularly healthful products; Coca-Cola was. Coke was stimulant, health tonic, and beverage.

Pemberton is known to have revealed the Coca-Cola formula to at least four persons. He told his partner/ bookkeeper, Frank M. Robinson. Apparently Pemberton told his son, Charles. (Later, at the behest of the Coca-Cola Company founder Asa G. Candler, Charles signed a document renouncing his right to use the formula.) And Pemberton told Willis E. Venable and George S. Lowndes, the two men who purchased the formula in July 1887.

A scarce five months later, Venable and Lowndes themselves sold out. They transmitted the formula and rights to Coca-Cola to Woolfolk Walker and Mrs. M. C. Dozier. Then in two separate transactions in 1888, Walker and Dozier sold their rights and the formula to Asa G. Candler. The same year saw the death of John Pemberton and a new marketing angle: mixing the syrup with carbonated water.

Candler was the first to recognize the potential of Coke. He equally recognized the importance of keeping the formula a secret. Unfortunately, at least seven people knew the Coke formula by the time Candler got it. At least some of them no longer had any particular incentive to preserve the secret.

Candler tied up one loose end by taking on Pemberton's old

Who Told Whom?
The Coca-Cola Formula

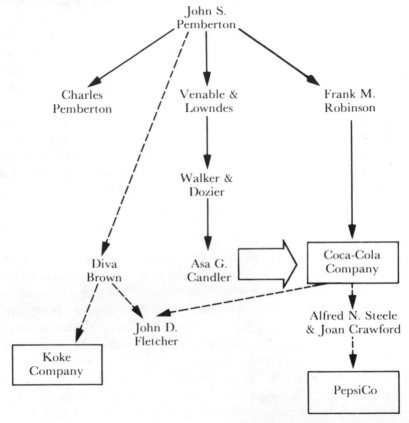

partner and one of the initiates, Frank Robinson, as his partner. Candler, evidently a more knowledgeable flavorist than Pemberton, soon revised the formula. By most accounts, Candler's changes were improvements. They also entitled Candler to claim that the increasing circle of outsiders who knew Pemberton's formula no longer knew the real Coca-Cola formula. In 1892, Candler, Robinson, and three others incorporated their operations as the Coca-Cola Company.

Candler instituted the shroud of secrecy that has since enveloped the formula. Candler and Robinson formed the first pair of initiates. Not until 1903 was anyone else allowed to make the syrup. The syrup was prepared in a locked laboratory, only Candler and Robinson having the combination to the door.

Shipments of ingredients were promptly deposited in the laboratory. There Candler or Robinson tore or scratched off the labels. They identified the ingredients by sight and smell. Lest a mail clerk learn the ingredients from the suppliers' bills, Candler opened all the company's mail himself. Likewise, Candler paid the bills himself to keep the accounting department from surmising any part of the secret. The invoices were kept in a locked file, and the only key to the file was kept on Candler's key ring, recounts Candler's son, Charles, in a 1950 biography, *Asa Griggs Candler.*

As the company got larger, Candler no longer could prepare all the syrup himself. In 1894 the first branch syrup plant was started in Dallas. Rather than relinquish the secret, Candler hit upon a scheme whereby people in other cities could prepare Coca-Cola syrup without knowing what was in it. The ingredients were numbered from 1 to 9, inclusive. Branch factory managers were told the relative proportions of the ingredients and the mixing procedure, but not the identities of the numbered ingredients. If the Dallas plant was running low on ingredient no. 6, it would order "merchandise no. 6" from Atlanta headquarters. Further to defy ready analysis, some of the merchandises were themselves mixtures of more basic ingredients.

To an extent, Candler was locking the barn after the horse had been stolen. It isn't clear who among the early initiates talked, but it seems someone must have.

For instance, there was Diva Brown, a woman who claimed that John Pemberton had sold her the Coca-Cola formula shortly before he died. True or not, Brown had somehow gleaned enough information about Coke's recipe to mix up passable imitations. She marketed Better Cola, Celery-Cola, Lime Cola, My-Coca, Vera-Coca, Vera Cola, and Yum-Yum in the southern states, claiming they were based on Pemberton's formula.

The Koke Company claimed to have gotten hold of Brown's formula upon her death in 1914 and thereby produced Koke, still another ersatz Coca-Cola. (For a long time, Coca-Cola neglected to trademark "Coke," fearing the nickname would encourage substitution. So the Koke Company was able to call its product Koke until stopped by a U.S. Supreme Court ruling in 1920.)

Meanwhile, John D. Fletcher, proprietor of a drink called "Coca and Cola," also claimed to have learned the Coke formula from Brown. He further claimed to have seen the formula in a Coca-Cola lawyer's briefcase during a protracted trial beginning in 1909, *United States* v. *Forty Barrels and Twenty Kegs of Coca-Cola*. Fletcher likewise was put out of business by a Coca-Cola lawsuit.

More problematic in the long run has been Pepsi-Cola, created by Caleb Bradham of New Bern, North Carolina, in 1898. The resemblance of the two drinks is all the more striking in view of the fact that kola nuts have little or nothing to do with the taste of either beverage (as we will see). Bradham did not have gas chromatography or other sophisticated analytic techniques. That he was able to produce such a convincing imitation of Coca-Cola suggests that he had heard something too.

In 1949 a top Coca-Cola Company executive, Alfred N. Steele, defected to PepsiCo. Steele's actress/wife, Joan Crawford, defected as well; Crawford had done endorsements for Coca-Cola. Steele was followed by several colleagues from Coca-Cola. After joining Pepsi, Steele boasted, "Their [Coca-Cola's] chemists know what's in our product, and our chemists know what's in theirs. Hell, I know both formulas."

Steele had been in Coca-Cola's marketing division, not in quality control. Whether Steele was one of the few formally initiated into knowledge of the full formula is questionable. But there can be little doubt about the contention that Pepsi knows Coke's formula (or most of it) and vice versa. There are ways of analyzing soft-drink flavorings, and it is hard to believe that both Coke and Pepsi haven't been thoroughly scrutinized by their competitors.

If Pepsi really knows Coke's secret, why hasn't it become a clone of the more popular drink? Most likely, Pepsi has considered the economics of duplicating Coke and decided against it. Being a larger company, Coca-Cola can produce its beverage at a lower unit cost than Pepsi could. In head-on competition with indistinguishable products, Pepsi would have to charge a higher price and eventually lose out. Instead, Pepsi produces a drink different enough from Coke that a segment of the public prefers it to Coke.

Secret Ingredient 7X

Today the Coca-Cola Company is nearly mute about Coke's flavoring ingredients. It no longer even mentions kola nuts in promotional literature. A short brochure, *You asked about soft drinks . . .* is bold enough to deny cocoa as an ingredient. (Some people confuse cocoa with coca.) If you write to ask if there is something truly repugnant in Coca-Cola, the company will, of course, deny it. Coca-Cola denies, for instance, pig blood, a rumored ingredient that has hurt sales to African Moslems. In E. J. Kahn, Jr.'s study of Coca-Cola, *The Big Drink,* he mentions the equally dubious rumor of peanuts as an ingredient—from former Coke president Robert W. Woodruff's peanut plantation.

Coke's label discloses, "Carbonated water, sugar, caramel color, phosphoric acid, natural flavorings, caffeine." Everything that makes Coke unique is subsumed under "natural flavorings."

The known ingredients can all be squared with Candler's system of numbered "merchandises." It is known that sugar is merchandise no. 1, caramel is no. 2, caffeine is no. 3, and phosphoric acid is no. 4. The water and carbonation apparently don't rate a merchandise number.

Coke's sugar used to be pure sucrose. Since 1980, syrup producers have been permitted to substitute high-fructose corn syrup for as much as 50 percent of the sugar. Some purists think the Coke with corn syrup doesn't taste as good. Before the change, former Coke Chairman J. Paul Austin knocked corn syrup: "It produces a chemical reaction with the Coca-Cola that throws the flavor off," he said in *Fortune.* Pepsi still uses sugar only. Not everyone notices the difference between sugar and corn syrup, but those who do apparently favor sugar. By one hypothesis, this slight tipping of the flavor scales in favor of Pepsi recently made it possible, for the first time, for Pepsi to gather "evidence" that most people favor Pepsi over Coke and use it in ads.

Coke's caramel is intended only as coloring. Virtually all Coke's brown color comes from the caramel. Coke's caramel is burnt cane or corn sugar.

Caffeine is the stimulant principle. Though it was Pemberton's idea to use natural extracts of kola nuts (containing caffeine) and coca leaves (containing cocaine) for stimulant effect, the amount of these ingredients in Coke is far too small to be significant. Nearly all the caffeine in Coke is chemically pure caffeine, a white powder.

Caffeine has a strong, bitter taste. The bitterness is largely covered up by the massive amounts of sugar used and the other flavorings. At the time of the *United States* v. *Forty Barrels and Twenty Kegs of Coca-Cola* trial, the caffeine used in Coke was refined from tea dust. During World War II, caffeine was scarce, and Coke's chemists toyed with the idea of synthesizing caffeine from bat guano. Coca-Cola executives rejected the plan on the grounds that the possible discovery of bat droppings as an "ingredient" of Coke would be too damaging. Coke may now be getting its caffeine from the guarana shrub of the Amazon basin; the seeds of these shrubs contain 5 percent caffeine.

The phosphoric acid provides a flat acidity. Other acids commonly used in soft drinks, such as citric or tartaric, suggest the acidity of specific fruits. Phosphoric acid doesn't. Pepsi lists both phosphoric and citric acids on its label, reflecting a more lemony acidity.

So much for merchandises 1 through 4. Several clues to the other ingredients come from the writings of Charles Howard Candler, son of the Coca-Cola Company's founder and an initiate. In his biography of his father, Candler tells of the merchandises: "The ingredients of Coca-Cola, throughout its early history, were categorized and referred to by numbers from one to nine inclusive . . ."

At another point, Candler tells where they bought the ingredients: "Among the suppliers of essential ingredients in the period under discussion were the E. Berghausen Chemical Company of Cincinnati; the Maywood Chemical Works, of Maywood, N. J.; the Monsanto Chemical Company of St. Louis; the Mallinckrodt Chemical Works, also of St. Louis; Harshaw, Fuller and Goodwin Company of Elyria, Ohio; and Procter & Gamble of Cincinnati."

In 1953, the younger Candler published another cola memoir, *Coca-Cola & Emory College*. In it he provides some cagey hints about the changes his father made in the Coca-Cola formula:

> Some of the very same people to whom he [Asa G. Candler] had paid hard-earned cash for what was then generally considered of little value, constantly plagued him by making and selling to unscrupulous dealers imitations of and for Coca-Cola, asserting that their concoctions were made from or based upon the original Coca-Cola formula. These unfair competitors may have had some knowledge of the Pemberton formula, but they knew absolutely nothing of the composition of *the* formula with which Asa G. Candler made Coca-

Cola. The Pemberton product did not have an altogether agreeable taste, it was unstable, it contained too many things, too much of some ingredients and too little of others.

Father's pharmaceutical knowledge convinced him that the formula had to be changed in certain particulars to improve the taste of the product, to insure its uniformity and its stability. Some of the ingredients were incompatible with others in the formula; the bouquet of several of the volatile essential oils previously used was adversely affected by some ingredients. Several needed materials, one notable for its preservative virtue, were added. The first thing he did was to discontinue the use of tin can containers for shipping. On account of the inclusion of a very desirable constituent in the formula, the use of tin cans was dangerous.

Here the "people to whom he had paid hard-earned cash" would include Walker, Dozier, and also the Pembertons, who retained an interest in Coca-Cola for several years. The second ingredient Candler hints at, the one that doesn't go with tin cans, is easy to guess. It's phosphoric acid. Phosphoric acid eats through tin, forming poisonous tin phosphate. (Currently, Coke uses stainless-steel containers.)

That means that the phosphoric acid was Candler's innovation and wasn't in the original formula. But Charles Candler says in the same book that the Pemberton formula included "an acid for zest." Perhaps this acid was one of the ingredients Candler took out of the formula. Or it could have been lime juice.

Lime juice is one of the ingredients that has been reported in chemical analyses of Coke. Several analyses of Coke were offered as evidence in the *United States* v. *Forty Barrels and Twenty Kegs of Coca-Cola* trial. In 1909 the federal government seized the latter quantity of Coca-Cola syrup en route from Atlanta to a bottling plant in Chattanooga and charged Coca-Cola with violation of the Pure Food Act. Trial and appeals ran about a decade. One analysis of the syrup claimed:

Caffein (grains per fluid ounce)	0.92–1.30
Phosphoric acid (H_3PO_4) (percent)	0.26–0.30
Sugar, total (percent)	48.86–58.00
Alcohol (percent by volume)	0.90–1.27
Caramel, glycerin, lime juice, essential oils, and plant extractives	Present
Water (percent)	34.00–41.00

Another analysis from the trial ran:

> Caffeine 0.20 per cent or 1.19 grains per ounce.
> Phos. Acid 0.19 per cent.
> Sugar 48.86 per cent.
> Alcohol 1.27 per cent.
> Caramel, glycerine,
> Lime Juice, oil of cassia
> Water about 41 per cent.

There seems little doubt that Coca-Cola contained lime juice circa 1909. To confirm its presence in Coke today, *Big Secrets* wrote the Coca-Cola Company asking about lime juice. Bonita Holder of Coca-Cola replied: "While we are unable to comment specifically on the various flavors utilized in Coca-Cola, I can nonetheless confirm for you that Coca-Cola contains no lime juice, or any fruit juice."

Lime juice is perishable and somewhat cloudy; it varies with each season's crop. Coke therefore might have wanted to replace it with a more stable substitute. A mixture of citric acid and some of the flavoring principles of lime juice (which are distinct from those found in the oil of lime peel) might have been substituted for the original lime juice without anyone noticing much of a change in the taste of Coca-Cola. Citrus juices are easy to fake. Coca-Cola produces such soft drinks as Hi-C Orange, Hi-C Lemonade, Hi-C Punch, and Hi-C Grape, which don't contain any fruit juice either.

The analyses mention three other ingredients: alcohol, glycerin, and oil of cassia. Evidently glycerin is the preservative Candler described. It is a customary ingredient in soft-drink syrups. It is believed to prevent separation of essential oils on standing.

Coke syrup is about 2 proof. The alcohol probably only enters in as a solvent for the "plant extractives." Oil of cassia seems to be one of the essential oils that provide Coke's flavoring. Cassia is a form of cinnamon, sometimes called Chinese cinnamon to distinguish it from true or Ceylon cinnamon. Most of the stick cinnamon sold in supermarkets is Ceylon cinnamon. Most of the cinnamon used in commercial baked goods such as coffee cakes is cassia.

Conspicuously absent from the above analyses is any mention of coca or kola. This was one of the main issues of the *United States*

v. *Forty Barrels and Twenty Kegs of Coca-Cola* trial. Coca leaves contain cocaine; ergo, it was claimed that Coca-Cola must either contain that recently outlawed drug, or the coca must have been dropped from the formula. In the latter case, the government charged, it was mislabeling to use "Coca" in the name. Further, it was charged the kola in Coca-Cola was an imposition—a trace ingredient added only so that the company could claim it was there. Thus the "Cola" part of the name was misleading, too.

Indeed, there is precious little coca or kola in Coca-Cola. None of the chemical analysts consulted at the trial were able to detect coca or kola. But there are traces of coca and kola present, in what Coca-Cola calls merchandise no. 5. At the time of the trial, merchandise no. 5 was manufactured by a contractor, the Schaeffer Alkaloid Works of Maywood, New Jersey. Its president, Dr. L. Schaeffer, described the manufacture of Coke's fifth ingredient:

> Q. Now, Doctor, do you make Merchandise No. 5 for the Coca-Cola Co.?
> A. Yes, sir.
> Q. From what substance do you make that Merchandise No. 5?
> A. Of the Coca leaf and the Cola nut, and of dilute alcohol sir.
> Q. What do you use the alcohol for, what is the purpose of putting in the alcohol?
> A. To extract from the bodies mentioned the extractive matter.
> Q. Do you use anything else in that compound except the extracts from the coca leaves and cola nuts and dilute alcohol?
> A. No, I do not use anything to speak of, or essentially.
> Q. Now just state the process, Dr. Schaeffer, by which you manufacture this Merchandise No. 5?
> A. The process consists of two parts. The first part is to decocanize the coca leaf, the second part is to use the decocanized coca leaf and cola nut, both of which are in powdered form, to make the infusion, that is, the same extract made by percolation with dilute alcohol. . . . The proportions which are used in the process are as follows: 380 lbs. of coca leaf, 125 lbs. of cola nuts and 900 gallons of dilute alcohol of about twenty per cent strength . . .

The cocaine was removed from the coca leaves by rinsing with toluol, a solvent. Cocaine dissolves in toluol; repeated rinsing leaches away the cocaine.

According to Dr. Schaeffer's testimony, there was wine in Coca-Cola. The alcohol used in making merchandise no. 5 was usually a mixture of California white wine and 95 percent commercial alcohol. But Dr. Schaeffer sometimes used an alcohol-water mixture "if California wine is too high in price. It is altogether a matter of price of the wine or of the alcohol."

Merchandise no. 5, according to testimony, was a dark, winey liquid. Several of the witnesses were given samples of merchandise no. 5. One thought it tasted and smelled no different from the wine it was made from. One Coca-Cola witness claimed it had the characteristic odor of coca but proved unable to describe the odor. Another witness said it smelled like toluol, the toxic solvent that isn't supposed to be present in the final product at all.

An experiment was performed for the benefit of the court. Coca-Cola made up a special batch of syrup containing no merchandise no. 5. Witnesses thought it tasted the same as the regular syrup.

In short, neither coca nor kola has much, if anything, to do with the taste of Coca-Cola. Both substances, in fact, have unpleasant, bitter flavors wholly unlike that of Coca-Cola.

Pemberton, remember, was concocting a medicinal syrup. Because his two active ingredients had unpleasant flavors, he masked them with other flavors—the way a codeine cough syrup might be cherry-flavored.

As it happened, Coca-Cola became successful for its flavor rather than for any medicinal value. Dozens of imitations sprang up, most with "Cola" in their name. Thus "cola" became the generic term for soft drinks similar to Coca-Cola. Most—though not all—of these imitations contained kola nuts. But as with Coke, the kola really didn't contribute to the flavor.

Cherry cough syrup tastes like cherries. The "cola" flavor tastes like . . . nothing familiar. That raises two possibilities. Cola flavor may come from an exotic substance, otherwise unknown to Western taste buds. Or it may be what the soft-drink industry calls a "fantasia" flavor, a new flavor created by the artful combination of other flavors.

The basics of cola flavor are no mystery. Pepsi, Royal Crown, and every supermarket chain know enough about the Coca-Cola formula to make good imitations. The cola flavor is a fantasia blend of three familiar flavors: citrus, cinnamon, and vanilla.

The prevailing philosophy, and certainly the philosophy behind Coca-Cola, is that these flavors should be blended so that none predominates and becomes identifiable in its own right. To the average palate, Coke does not taste like citrus, cinnamon, or vanilla.

But some of the cheaper, supermarket house-brand colas taste slightly of cinnamon or vanilla. Pepsi has a more lemony taste than Coke—and Pepsi Light advertises its lemon flavor.

Here citrus means the oils pressed from the peels. The oils are responsible for most of the smell of citrus fruits but taste nothing like the juice. All citrus oils are very bitter by themselves. Diluted in a soft-drink emulsion, they acquire a more pleasant taste.

All three familiar citrus fruits—oranges, lemons, and limes— are probably used in Coca-Cola. At any rate, Pepsi-Cola, which is more candid about its formula, admits to orange, lemon, and lime oils (as well as vanilla and kola nuts) in a brochure, *Pepsi-Cola: Quality in Every Drop.* The theory always has been that Coke has relatively more orange and less lemon than Pepsi. Food writer Roy Andries de Groot tells of plying a Coca-Cola Company executive with rum-and-Cokes to get an admission. According to de Groot, the executive uh-huhed the Coke:orange/Pepsi:lemon analysis.

How are these ingredients combined? The sources *Big Secrets* consulted pointed to a book, *Food Flavorings: Composition, Manufacture, and Use,* by Joseph Merory (second edition, 1968). Merory was the founder and president of Merory Food Flavors, a small flavoring supplier in Fairfield, New Jersey. To the horror of many of his colleagues, Merory published dozens of standard flavoring formulations in the book, drawing on his own experience and what was common knowledge in the flavoring industry. One of his recipes, designated MF 241, is a "cola flavor" that seems to be Merory's version of Coca-Cola. Another recipe, "Cola Syrup" MF 234, suggests Pepsi.

The seeming Coca-Cola recipe, MF 241, is for a cola flavor, which must be mixed with sugar syrup and phosphoric acid to produce cola syrup. Cola syrup in turn must be mixed with carbonated water to produce the finished drink. Merory's recipe specifies these ingredients:

> Caramel (32 fluid ounces)
> Lime juice (32 fluid ounces)
> Glycerin (16 fluid ounces)
> Alcohol (95 percent) (12 fluid ounces)
> Cola flavor base (12 fluid ounces)
> Kola nut extract (12 fluid ounces)
> Caffeine solution (2 ounces of caffeine in
>   10 fluid ounces of water)
> Vanilla extract (2 fluid ounces)

These are mixed to produce 128 ounces (1 gallon) of cola flavor. Four ounces of this cola flavor, plus .5 fluid ounce of diluted phosphoric acid (one part 85 percent phosphoric acid to seven parts water), are used to flavor a gallon of sugar syrup. The composition of the cola flavor base and the kola nut extract are given in accompanying recipes.

This recipe suggests the identities of the unknown merchandises. Merchandise no. 1, sugar, is the syrup to which the cola flavor is added. Nos. 2 and 3, caramel and caffeine, are in the recipe, caffeine in a water solution. No. 4, phosphoric acid, is added to the sugar syrup. No. 5, in Coca-Cola's recipe, is coca and kola extract in an alcohol-water solution. This corresponds to two ingredients in the Merory recipe: the kola nut extract and the 95 percent alcohol. The kola nut extract is to be prepared according to another Merory recipe, MF 237. This requires that kola nuts be extracted with a solvent, propylene glycol, most of which is then distilled off. Water is added, so the result is a water-based extract of kola. Were alcohol added to this extract, you'd have a sort of merchandise no. 5 (without the coca, though). Of course, the alcohol and kola extract can be treated as separate ingredients—which is how Merory lists them.

There are four remaining ingredients in Merory's list—and four remaining merchandises of the nine Candler claimed. Merory's four are lime juice, glycerin, a cola flavor base, and vanilla extract. Of these, the first two were reported in lab analyses of Coke (though Coke now denies lime juice). The last, vanilla extract, is a generally acknowledged component of the cola flavor.

It is tempting if not compelling to identify these four with merchandises nos. 6 through 9. We can't be sure that Coca-Cola doesn't mix together glycerin and vanilla extract, say, and call it merchandise no. 6. But since glycerin and vanilla extract must be prepared or purchased separately, it makes sense to consider them as separate merchandises. The cola flavor base is a composite product—a mixture of citrus and spice oils in alcohol. It includes all the essential oils used in the cola. Because essential oils are powerful flavorings and must be diluted, it makes sense to mix them up in a large batch (to ensure a uniform product) and to draw from this premixed batch as needed. The oil mixture would then be regarded as a single ingredient.

The oil mixture may be the mysterious ingredient 7X of Coke lore. Merchandise 7X is the most secret of Coke's secret ingredients. The "X" has never been explained; 7X seems to be simply merchandise no. 7. It might make sense if there was a merchandise no. 7 composed of many ingredients, all given letters: 7A, 7B, 7C . . . 7X. But no one associated with Coke has ever alluded to any of the other members of this hypothetical series. What's more, we know that 7X is itself a composite ingredient. Charles Candler writes of making "a batch of merchandise 7X" while his father supervised the measuring and mixing.

Certainly the essential oil mixture is the most important component of a cola's flavor. The "cola flavor base" referred to above is given in another Merory recipe, MF 238. It is made from the following:

Cold-pressed California lemon oil (46.80 grams)
Orange oil (24.84 grams)
Distilled lime oil (14.20 grams)
Cassia or cinnamon oil (10.65 grams)
Nutmeg oil (3.50 grams)
Neroli oil ["can be omitted," says Merory] (0.01 gram)

If the aforementioned analysis presented at the *United States* v. *Forty Barrels and Twenty Kegs of Coca-Cola* trial was correct, it is cassia rather than true cinnamon oil that is used in Coca-Cola. Nutmeg is a likely minor component of the Coca-Cola flavor base, for aside from Merory's equivocal endorsement of it here, it has been claimed detected in outside chemical analyses. Neroli is an oil distilled from the blossoms of the bitter orange tree. It forms only one part in ten thousand of Merory's oil mixture, though. That and the difficulty of distinguishing citrus oil in chemical analysis make it hard to say if neroli oil is in Coca-Cola. According to the Merory recipe for flavor base, the above mixture of oils (100 grams) is mixed with 11 fluid ounces of 95 percent alcohol and shaken. Five ounces of water are added, and the mixture is left to stand for twenty-four hours. A cloudy layer of terpenes will develop; only the clear part of the mixture is taken off and used in recipe MF 241.

There may be other ingredients in the Coca-Cola oil mixture. In *The Big Drink,* E. J. Kahn, Jr., mentions the possibility of lavender as an ingredient. The alternate Merory cola recipe, which uses citric acid and less orange oil, suggesting a Pepsi-like product, includes coriander in lieu of nutmeg. (Coriander is a spice found in Danish pastries.) Perhaps there is a trace of coriander in Coca-Cola. In another of the occasional breaches of industry closemouthedness, flavorist A. W. Noling published a pamphlet on colas in 1952. The *Hurty Peck Pamphlet on Cola* attributed the secret of cola flavor to extracts of decocanized coca leaves and kola nuts, oils of lime, lemon, orange, cassia, nutmeg, neroli, cinnamon, and coriander, and lime juice and vanilla. Noling's analysis seems to have been directed specifically at Coca-Cola. Among modern cola drinks, only Coca-Cola is known to use the coca leaves.

The proportions in the accompanying recipe are based on the analyses of Coke quoted above and Merory's recipes. The amount of caffeine agrees with that stated in Coca-Cola's *So you asked about soft drinks* . . . pamphlet; this is about a third of the caffeine found in the trial analyses.

The following recipe produces a gallon of syrup very similar to Coca-Cola's. Mix 2,400 grams of sugar with just enough water to dissolve (high-fructose corn syrup may be substituted for half the sugar). Add 37 grams of caramel, 3.1 grams of caffeine, and 11 grams of phosphoric acid. Extract the cocaine from 1.1 grams of coca leaf (*Truxillo* growth of coca preferred) with toluol; discard the cocaine extract. Soak the coca leaves and kola nuts (both finely powdered; 0.37 gram of kola nuts) in 22 grams of 20 percent alcohol. California white wine fortified to 20 percent strength was used as the soaking solution circa 1909, but Coca-Cola may have switched to a simple water/alcohol mixture. After soaking, discard the coca and the kola and add the liquid to the syrup. Add 30 grams of lime juice (a former ingredient, evidently, that Coca-Cola now denies) or a substitute such as a water solution of citric acid and sodium citrate at lime-juice strength. Mix together 0.88 gram of lemon oil, 0.47 gram of

Coca-Cola: The Real Things?

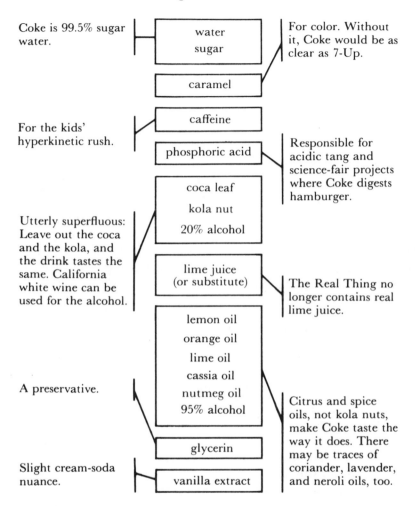

Coke is 99.5% sugar water.

water

sugar

For color. Without it, Coke would be as clear as 7-Up.

caramel

For the kids' hyperkinetic rush.

caffeine

phosphoric acid

Responsible for acidic tang and science-fair projects where Coke digests hamburger.

coca leaf

kola nut

20% alcohol

Utterly superfluous: Leave out the coca and the kola, and the drink tastes the same. California white wine can be used for the alcohol.

lime juice (or substitute)

The Real Thing no longer contains real lime juice.

lemon oil

orange oil

lime oil

cassia oil

A preservative.

nutmeg oil

95% alcohol

Citrus and spice oils, not kola nuts, make Coke taste the way it does. There may be traces of coriander, lavender, and neroli oils, too.

glycerin

Slight cream-soda nuance.

vanilla extract

orange oil, 0.27 gram of lime oil, 0.20 gram of cassia (Chinese cinnamon) oil, 0.07 gram of nutmeg oil, and if desired, traces of coriander, lavender, and neroli oils, and add to 4.9 grams of 95 percent alcohol. Shake. Add 2.7 grams of water to the alcohol/oil mixture and let stand for twenty-four hours at about 60° F. A cloudy layer will separate. Take off the clear part of the liquid only and add to the syrup. Add 19 grams of glycerin (from vegetable sources, not hog fat, so the drink can be sold to Orthodox Jews and Moslems) and 1.5 grams of vanilla extract. Add water (treated with chlorine) to make 1 gallon of syrup.

Yield (used to flavor carbonated water): 128 6.5-ounce bottles.

The amount of kola in this recipe—or in any cola—is tiny. Some colas are reported to contain none at all. By this recipe, a gallon of cola syrup is made from 0.37 gram of kola nut. But a gallon is 128 fluid ounces, and each ounce can flavor a bottle of finished, carbonated beverage. So the amount of kola nut used in making a bottle of cola drink is about 3 milligrams. That tiny speck is merely soaked in alcohol and then discarded, only the alcohol going into the cola syrup.

Many Coca-Cola drinkers swear that the drink tastes different in various parts of the country. Coke's standard answer is to blame the mineral content of the water used by the bottling plants. (Now that the syrup plants have the option of using corn syrup for part of the sugar, the Coke in regions where they do use corn syrup ought to taste different from—probably not as good as—the Coke where only cane sugar is used.) Where soda fountains still make Coke from syrup, another variable is the "throw"—the amount of carbonated water added to the syrup. Southerners tend to like Coke on the syrupy side.

Is There Cocaine in Coca-Cola?

Coca-Cola was not always alone in its use of coca. There were coca elixirs and beverages before there were colas. Until 1903, Coca-Cola contained the full cocaine content of its coca extract. Since then, Coca-Cola has taken great pains to remove the cocaine from the coca leaves before they go into merchandise no. 5. According to one source, there were sixty-nine imitations of Coca-Cola still containing measurable cocaine in 1909.

One version of the chestnut about putting an aspirin in Coca-Cola says that the cocaine is thus precipitated. (The more usual version holds that the aspirin-Coke mixture acts as a Mickey, the opposite of what would be expected from cocaine.) Of course, the Coca-Cola Company bristles at any suggestion that there might still be cocaine in the drink.

Even before 1903, the amount of cocaine in Coca-Cola was trifling. One analysis put the cocaine content of an ounce of Coca-Cola syrup—in the pre-extraction days—at 0.04 grain (2.6 milligrams).

That's not much. In small doses, cocaine has roughly the stimulant effect of a dose of caffeine ten times larger. A milligram of cocaine might have the effect of 10 milligrams of caffeine, and so forth. So the cocaine in an ounce of the old syrup had the stimulant effect of about 26 milligrams of caffeine. In comparison, a cup of tea contains about 60 milligrams of caffeine.

By the same analysis, the old Coke syrup contained about 1.21 grains (78 milligrams) of caffeine. Even when Coke contained measurable amounts of cocaine, most of its stimulant effect must have been from the caffeine.

Figure that a line of uncut cocaine is about 50 milligrams. Then it would have taken nearly 20 ounces of the old Coca-Cola syrup (or 20 of the 6.5-ounce bottles of carbonated beverage) to represent an equivalent amount of cocaine. Anyone trying to consume that much would have gotten sick from the caffeine, phosphoric acid, or sugar.

From time to time, various chemists and government agencies have wondered if there is any residual cocaine in Coca-Cola even yet. In 1912, nine years after the switch to decocanized coca leaves, a Canadian government study found no cocaine in Coca-Cola syrup.

In 1972 Dr. Norman Farnsworth of the University of Illinois, Chicago, had graduate students test Coke and other colas for cocaine. A gas-chromatography "peak" near that expected for cocaine was found. To confirm the apparent finding, Farnsworth's group added cocaine to a sample of Coca-Cola and retested. This time there were two peaks—meaning that something other than cocaine was causing the first peak. A scientific paper reporting the original finding was hastily shelved.

So jittery was the Coca-Cola Company on hearing of the results that it funded further research to find the cause of the spurious peak—lest a less careful researcher might report the "cocaine." Farnsworth finally concluded the peak was due to a polymer formed from the ammonia used in the gas chromatography.

You can make a strong argument that there must be *some* cocaine in Coca-Cola nonetheless. The decocanization process used on the coca leaves that go into Coke is similar to the decaffeination of coffee. A solvent is passed through the leaves repeatedly, leaching away a little more cocaine each time. So it is with the caffeine in decaffeinated coffee. But no coffee producer claims its decaffeinated coffee is entirely free from caffeine. A brand that advertises itself as 98 percent caffeine-free contains only 2 percent of the caffeine of regular coffee. For all practical purposes, that's good enough.

Coke's decocanization is good enough, too, as far as the drug laws are concerned. No one suggests that there is enough cocaine in a bottle of Coke to have any physiological effect whatsoever. But it's quite another thing to assert that there is no cocaine in Coca-Cola. A molecule of cocaine, the smallest possible amount, weighs 0.000000000000000000504 milligram. If an ounce of the old syrup contained 2.6 milligrams of cocaine, then it must have contained about 5 quintillion (5,000,000,000,000,000,000) molecules of cocaine.

Does Coke's decocanization process catch every last one of those 5 quintillion molecules? Surely not. If it removed 99 percent of them—which would be pretty good—there would still be a whopping 50 quadrillion molecules left.

Even if the Coca-Cola Company invested in a hypothetical superdecocanizer capable of removing 99.99999999 percent of the cocaine (a pointless waste of money, given the insignificant role of coca extract in the finished beverage), there would still be millions and millions of molecules of cocaine left in every bottle of Coke. As long as Coca-Cola is made from coca leaves, it can hardly avoid containing cocaine.

4·

Uncolas

Dr Pepper

It's easier to say what isn't in Dr Pepper than what is. Though Dr Pepper is sometimes categorized as a cherry cola, the Dr Pepper Company denies both cherry and kola flavorings. Likewise, almost everything that has been rumored to be in Dr Pepper isn't in it. There is no black pepper, chili pepper, bell pepper, or peppermint. And no prune juice.

The formula contains twenty-three ingredients and is locked in two bank vaults. Four persons know it. Company CEO W. W. Clements said he saw the formula once but didn't understand it. The only surprise on the label ingredient panel is lactic acid. This is what gives sour milk its bite. If you hold some Dr Pepper in your mouth a few minutes before swallowing, there is a slight yogurtlike note.

Dr Pepper smells. The honeysuckle-sweet odor is prominent when the drink is served cold, overpowering when served hot. Industry opinion holds that vanilla or vanillin is a prime ingredient in Dr Pepper, responsible in part for that smell. In reply to a query from *Big Secrets*, a Dr Pepper Company vice president confirmed that synthetic vanillin is an ingredient. Synthetics figure prominently in Dr Pepper's fantasia blend. The label credits "artificial and natural flavoring," the word order implying that there are more artificial than natural flavors in Dr Pepper. At any rate, Dr Pepper is the only soft drink of the big four to be artificially flavored.

In 1981 W. W. Clements told a *Los Angeles Times* reporter that he used to fear theft of the Dr Pepper formula. "Then I got to thinking," recalled Clements. "Why would anyone go to all that trouble just to produce another Dr Pepper? Then I quit worrying."

Hires Root Beer

Root beer used to be a fermented, slightly alcoholic brew flavored with bruised sassafras bark, wintergreen bark, and sarsaparilla root. Hires bears but a faint resemblance to the original product. It is made like a cola—lots of sugar, caramel for the brown color, artificial carbonation. Its flavor comes mainly from a secret flavoring extract that may not contain any of the traditional trio of root beer flavorings. Predominant in most modern root beer formulations is methyl salicylate, an oily synthetic compound also present naturally in wintergreen. Much cheaper than natural oil of wintergreen—and by most accounts, an agreeable substitute—methyl salicylate is a likely component of Hires. A typical modern-type recipe for root beer flavoring in Merory's *Food Flavorings* calls for methyl salicylate along with oil of northern birch, oil or star anise (or synthetic anethol as a substitute), ginger oleoresin, cold-pressed lemon oil, ginger oil, citral (a synthetic also present in lemons), and coriander. How does Hires create its foam? If it's like most root beer producers, it uses the sap of the desert yucca tree. Root beer is no more highly carbonated than a cola, but something in the yucca sap keeps the bubbles from breaking.

Moxie

Moxie's secret formula once overshadowed Coca-Cola's. In the 1920s Moxie outsold Coke and may have been the biggest-selling trademarked soft drink in the world. Then sugar prices went up, and the company decided to use its advertising budget to buy sugar instead. Bad decision. People forgot about Moxie except in its New England stronghold. Now the syrup is made in Doraville, Georgia, strangely enough, though the drink is rarely seen except in Maine and Massachusetts. Moxie looks like a cola; it tastes (and smells) like root beer heavily laced with Angostura Bitters.

The one flavoring credited on Moxie's label, gentian root extract, is in Angostura Bitters as well. The Moxie Company once claimed twenty other flavorings besides the gentian. Cinchona alkaloids, responsible for the bitterness of tonic water, used to be listed as an ingredient on the fountain syrup label. Sassafras was another alleged ingredient.

Never identified is the mysterious "simple sugarcane-like plant grown near the equator and farther south" touted in Moxie's early advertising. The plant, "discovered accidentally by Lieut. Moxie," according to the old label, was claimed to be a remedy for "brain and nervous exhaustion; loss of manhood, imbecility and . . . softening of the brain." Neither gentian, cinchona, nor sassafras is anything like sugarcane. A 1903 book, *The Secrets of the Specialists*, claimed the secret ingredient was oats. Author Dr. Dale Covey found Moxie to be a "decoction of oats made into a syrup and flavored with sassafras and wintergreen." But oats are hardly sugarcane-like or equatorial. Be that as it may, old Moxie labels depicted a woman carrying grain (oats?) on her shoulder.

7-Up

This is the only major soft drink with no secrets. 7-Up has six ingredients and reveals them to anyone who cares to know. They are carbonated water, sugar (corn syrup substitution allowed), citric acid, sodium citrate, lemon oil, and lime oil.

Vernors

You either think Vernors is the champagne of ginger ales, or you think it has a weird, off taste and wish you'd bought the regular stuff. The company notes sales are exceptionally strong during the Christmas and Easter seasons, when the drink is used to glaze turkeys and hams. The first batch of Vernors was prepared in 1865. Vernors is thus older than Coca-Cola (1886), Dr Pepper (1885), and Moxie (1876). Inventor James Vernor flavored his drink with the contents of a wooden keg of secret ingredients he had left stewing in Detroit before joining the Union army in 1861. Ever since, ingredients have been aged for four years in forty-seven-gallon oak barrels. Vernors contains three types of ginger and seventeen other ingredients, according to the company. Pre-

sumably, part of the taste seeps in from the oak. Even regular ginger ales contain flavorings other than ginger. A Merory recipe for
ginger ale flavoring calls for lime, lemon, and orange oil. Though
never confirmed, citrus oils likely figure in the recipe for Vernors
too. The "hot" taste of Vernors may be due to hot peppers, another sometime ingredient of ginger ales.

Yoo-Hoo

Yoo-Hoo is not a chocolated nondairy creamer; the label claims
milk and whey. The chocolate flavor is from natural cocoa, synthetic vanillin, and some unspecified natural flavorings. Yoo-Hoo
is made in part from seaweed (the "carrageenan gum" they hope
you won't notice on the label). Coconut oil replaces the fat lost by
watering down the whey-milk mixture. Whatever's in Yoo-Hoo, a
lot of it precipitates out to form a three-tone layer of sediment at
the bottom of the bottle or can. From bottom to top, the layers are
dark brown, light brown, and burnt sienna.

Industry sources say Yoo-Hoo owes its open-ended shelf life to a
special steam sterilization process. Sterilization takes place after
the bottles are filled and capped but before labels are applied.
Unopened Yoo-Hoo is as sterile as a Band-Aid; as long as it's
sealed, it can't go sour.

5·

Liqueurs and Bitters

Formulas for many aperitifs, bitters, and liqueurs are still family affairs. Secrets are handed down on deathbeds, with the curtains drawn and the servants in town on errands. The longevity of these arcane elixirs has given outsiders plenty of time to puzzle out the recipes. Outside chemists' best guesses follow.

Angostura Bitters
Port of Spain, Trinidad
90 proof

Angostura Bitters are the family secret of the Siegerts of Trinidad, descendents of Dr. J.G.B. Siegert. The family is said to eat their food heavily laced with the bitters. The German Dr. Siegert served in the army of Simón Bolívar on the South American mainland. In 1824 Dr. Siegert invented the bitters as a tonic for Bolívar's army. The bitters proved a success, and Siegert secretly moved the family business to the more stable political turf of Trinidad. For a long time after its creation, the recipe was communicated only by word of mouth. At last report, the recipe has been written down, the paper torn in two, and the halves locked in separate bank vaults.

Although Angostura Bitters enter into recipes for Manhattans, Old-Fashioneds, Rob Roys, and countless other mixed-drink recipes, few have any idea what's in Angostura Bitters. In *Islands in the Stream*, Ernest Hemingway likens the flavor to varnish. The odor suggests plum pudding. Taken straight up (as the label suggests to stimulate the appetite or relieve flatulence), Angostura Bitters are thoroughly unpleasant. The taste is so bad that Angostura Bitters are exempted from the alcoholic-beverage tax. The reasoning is that no one could down enough of the 90-proof bitters to get drunk.

The label admits only three ingredients: water, alcohol, and gentian. Gentian is a wild flower with a bitter root. The rest is "harmless vegetable flavoring extractives and vegetable coloring matter." There seems not to be any sugar.

Angostura bark is to Angostura Bitters what cocaine is to Coca-Cola. The label eagerly denies angostura bark as an ingredient. According to the label, the bitters aren't named after angostura bark, but rather after the town of Angostura, Venezuela (since renamed Ciudad Bolívar). Yet the *Encyclopaedia Britannica* and other older sources claim angostura bark is—or was—the bitters' principal flavoring.

What's wrong with angostura bark? Angostura is a small tree from northern Brazil and adjacent Venezuela. Its bark is spicy-bitter and was used medicinally. Then scandal erupted when someone discovered that the "angostura bark" of commerce was often adulterated with the poisonous bark of the strychnine tree. Presumably, Angostura Bitters were made from this same contaminated angostura bark. The family has always refused to discuss ingredients, but apparently Angostura Bitters were hastily reformulated to exclude angostura bark.

Now gentian is mostly responsible for the bitter-Moxie flavor of the bitters. According to economic botanist Julia F. Morton, Sc.D., of the University of Miami (Fla.), two other flavorings are bitter orange peel and galangal. Citrus peel enters into many other bitter drinks, such as Campari. Galangal is a pungent root spice, related to ginger, that otherwise turns up in Indonesian cooking. Another widely suspected ingredient is cloves.

The most complete published breakdown of Angostura Bitters appears in the *Source Book of Flavors* by Henry B. Heath (Westport, Conn.: AVI Publishing Co., 1981). Heath's Angostura recipe is not a complete chemical analysis, but it is an expert guess, based on the best available information, about what goes into Angostura Bitters. Heath's recipe uses angostura bark rather than gentian and thus seems to simulate the old-style bitters. In order of declining quantity, it calls for:

10 parts	Angostura Bark
4 parts	Bitter Orange Fruit
4 parts	Bitter Orange Peel
4 parts	Cinnamon Bark
4 parts	Tonka Beans
3 parts	Cloves
2 parts	Calisaya Bark
2 parts	Cardamon
2 parts	Carob
2 parts	Ginger
2 parts	Lemon Peel
1 part	Galangal
1 part	Zedoary

According to Heath, all ingredients are percolated with 50 percent alcohol. Two ounces of the resulting concentrated extract are used to flavor a gallon of the finished product.

What about the bright pink color Angostura Bitters impart to gin? It must come from a vegetable dye. None of the flavoring ingredients have much color when diluted to final strength.

Benedictine
Fécamp, France
80 proof

Benedictine boasts the oldest secret recipe of any popular food or drink. It was invented at the Benedictine Abbey of Fécamp by Dom Bernardo Vincelli in 1510. For centuries the recipe was concocted only by monks. Now the formula is in the more secular hands of a family-owned corporation. It is still made at Fécamp, though in a replica of the original monastery. According to *Grossman's Guide*, only three people are ever permitted to know the complete recipe.

Benedictine fairly taunts its imitators with a Salon de Contrefaçons (Hall of Counterfeits) at its distillery. The Salon is a massive collection of the hundreds of imitation "Benedictines" produced around the globe.

The taste of true Benedictine is agreeable, sweet, and distinctive. The alcohol base is brandy. It is known that there are many ingredients; that they mixed in more than one step; and that the liqueur is aged for four years before bottling.

Fenaroli's Handbook of Flavor Ingredients, an industry bible, argues knowingly that the gist of Benedictine flavor is three ingredients: citrus, angelica, and juniper berries. Angelica is a sweet, licorice-flavored herb of northern Europe; juniper berries, from the common shrub, are also used to flavor gin. Most flavor chemists agree with the *Fenaroli* assessment, but no one doubts that many other trace ingredients are used as well. Peppermint, cloves, and balm (sold in health-food stores for brewing a lemon-scented herb tea) are widely suspected.

In *Food Flavorings*, Joseph Merory gave a recipe for imitation Benedictine with twenty flavorings. The ingredients in the left-hand column below are soaked in thirty-three gallons of 40 percent alcohol for four days. Twenty gallons are removed for later use. The ingredients in the right-hand column are added to the remaining mixture. A day later, this entire mixture is distilled. The first ten gallons of distillate are mixed with the twenty gallons of filtered extract set aside on the fourth day. The result, a 100-proof flavoring, is mixed with sugar syrup, water, and brandy to yield the correct flavor intensity, sweetness, and proof.

lbs.		*lbs.*	
7.5	Angelica Root	4.5	Angelica Root
2.5	Balm	4.5	Calamus
2.5	Mugwort	4.5	Gentian
2.5	Peppermint	4.5	Mace
2.25	Valencia Orange Peel	2.25	Spanish Orange Peel
2.0	Coriander	1.875	Cardamon Seeds
1.5	Calamus	1.875	Cloves
1.25	Hyssop (Herbs)	1.875	Roman Chamomile
1.25	Hyssop (Leaves)	1.25	Thyme
1.25	Thyme		
1.0	Arnica Blossom		
0.875	Musk Seed		
0.5	Cardamon Seeds		
0.5	Cassia		
0.25	Cloves		
0.15	Nutmeg		

Campari
Milan, Italy
48 proof

Gaspare Campari's crimson aperitif is sold as a bottled carbonated beverage in Europe. The product sold in the United States is the "syrup" from which Campari soda can be made. Chemical analysis shows that syrup is the right word. By weight, about 23 percent of Campari is sugar—a sucrose megadose for a drink that does not, to the first-time drinker, taste sweet at all. Whatever is in Campari, it is bitter enough to mask a cloying base. An even sweeter version of Campari is sold as an after-dinner cordial.

There is no question that citrus oils are the primary flavorings. They are probably bitter orange, with some lemon and possibly some sweet orange. There is less agreement on the other flavorings. According to Guido Zamarini, a flavor chemist who produced a Campari imitation in Mexico, Campari's chiaroscuro undertones come from rhubarb and cocoa. Zamarini's formula used rhubarb, quinine, oils of bitter orange, sweet orange, and lemon, cocoa, and gentian.

Heath's *Source Book of Flavors* includes an "Italian Bitters" recipe—evidently intended as an approximation to Campari—in which angelica and other herbs back up the citrus. The recipe uses:

1¼ lb.	Bitter Orange Peel	12 oz.	Wormwood Leaves
1 lb.	Angelica Root	8 oz.	Cinnamon
1 lb.	Buckbean Leaves	7 oz.	Cloves
1 lb.	Lemon Peel	5 oz.	Marjoram
12 oz.	Anise	5 oz.	Sage
12 oz.	Calamus	5 oz.	Thyme
12 oz.	Fennel	2 oz.	Rosemary
12 oz.	Orris Root		

All are percolated with 50 percent alcohol; 2 ounces flavor a gallon of sweetened alcohol/water mixture. Campari's color apparently is a combination of red carmine and brown caramel.

Chartreuse
Voiron, France
80 proof (yellow) and 110 proof (green)

The secret formula for Chartreuse was a gift from the Maréchal d'Estrées to the monastery of the Grande Chartreuse near Grenoble in 1607. It is still produced by Carthusian monks. It was slightly reformulated once—in 1757, by Brother Gérome Manbec. The secret almost fell out of the order's control in the early part of this century. Legal problems forced the Carthusian fathers to flee France in 1901. All the order's property, including the recipe, was to have been sold at auction. No copy of the recipe remained in France, however. The exiled fathers produced Chartreuse in Tarragona, Spain. After protracted litigation in France, the Carthusians were able to return to Voiron and resume production in France.

Green, yellow, and white (colorless) Chartreuse is produced. The green and yellow colors, it's suspected, are as artificial as those of lemon and lime Kool-Aid. Green Chartreuse is more alcoholic than the yellow form. Some tasters claim slight flavor differences as well. Others think the "differences" are nothing more than the suggestive power of the two colors. Taste as well as chemical analysis show that both forms are ungodly sweet: about 28 percent sugar by weight in the yellow variety. A 750-milliliter bottle of yellow Chartreuse contains about half a pound of sugar.

Is Chartreuse a rip-off of Benedictine? Connoisseurs charge the two liqueurs are similar. (Presumably Chartreuse has been spared display in the Salon de Contrefaçons.) The comparison is more striking if you close your eyes and have someone give you sips of Benedictine and yellow Chartreuse. No one knows exactly how the Maréchal d'Estrées came by his recipe, but his gift came a century after the invention of Benedictine.

Like Benedictine, Chartreuse has a brandy base. *Fenaroli's Handbook* contends that the basic Chartreuse flavor is a mélange of citrus, angelica, juniper berries, anise, and wormwood. Three of these five were listed as the primary flavorings of Benedictine. Anise provides a second, licoricelike note, not unlike angelica; wormwood, a constituent of vermouth, provides bitterness. The *Fenaroli's Handbook* recipe for Chartreuse flavoring uses essential oils rather than raw spices and herbs:

60 parts	Lemon Oil
20 parts	Anethol (main component of anise oil)
15 parts	Juniper Oil
7.1 parts	Clary Sage Oil
4 parts	Hyssop Oil
3 parts	Bitter Orange Oil
3 parts	Mint Oil
3 parts	Petitgrain Oil
2.5 parts	Coriander Oil
2.1 parts	Angelica Oil
2.1 parts	Mace Oil
2.1 parts	Wormwood Oil
2 parts	Sweet Orange Oil
1 part	Caraway Oil
1 part	Cinnamon Oil
Trace	Lavender Oil

One part of this oil mixture flavors about five thousand parts of liqueur. This is a "compound" Chartreuse flavor. *Fenaroli's Handbook* suggests that the anise note should be more pronounced in the yellow form and subdued in the green.

Fernet Branca
New York
78 proof

Fernet Branca is a hangover cure and sometime ingredient of mixed drinks. It was devised by a Dr. Fernet, a Swede, as a tonic against cholera. The biting, medicinal taste gives no clue to its composition. The color is a murky sepia-black.

The label lists nine ingredients: aloes, gentian, zedoary, cinchona, calumba, rhubarb, angelica, chamomile, and saffron. This sounds like enough ingredients, but some authorities suspect there are others, not mentioned. For one thing, Fernet Branca smells like mint. None of the label ingredients smell much like mint, and it is questionable if their odors could combine to simulate mint. *Fenaroli's Handbook* maintains that mint essential oil is an ingredient. *Fenaroli's* further claims calamus, centaury, imperatoria, larch agaric (a mushroom growing around larch trees), St. Johnswort, and myrrh (as in the Bible, a hardened, pungent sap from an African tree) as ingredients of Fernet Branca or Fernet imitations. No citrus is used, says *Fenaroli's*.

Priciest of Fernet's ingredients is saffron. Better known for its color than flavor, saffron has a pungent, bitter taste. It sells for over a hundred dollars a pound. But according to a recipe in Merory's *Food Flavorings*, a scant 50 grams of saffron suffice for a 100-liter batch of imitation Fernet. If this approximates the proportion of saffron in genuine Fernet Branca, the cost of saffron per bottle is on the order of ten cents.

Fernet's inky color comes from a larger-than-usual dose of caramel coloring.

Grand Marnier
Paris, France
80 proof

Grand Marnier is an orange liqueur, yet it tastes different from generic orange Curaçao-type liqueurs. Part of the reason is the cognac base. Cheaper brands use flavorless "neutral spirits." The other difference is a secret list of background flavorings. According to a recipe in *Food Flavorings*, the principal secret ingredient is peppermint. Merory's recipe for "Grand 'M'-Type Flavor" uses more noncitrus than citrus flavorings:

4750 gm.	Bitter Orange Peel
2500 gm.	Peppermint
2250 gm.	Sweet Orange Peel
1750 gm.	Lemon Peel
1500 gm.	Coriander Seed
1500 gm.	Curaçao Orange Peel
1500 gm.	Ginger
1500 gm.	Orange Blossoms
1075 gm.	Cloves
875 gm.	Angelica Seed
875 gm.	Cinnamon
250 gm.	Cardamon
100 gm.	Saffron
100 gm.	Tonka Beans

Cointreau is believed to use many of the same ingredients but is prepared less sweet.

PART TWO

Everything You Owe Is Wrong

F ace it: Of healthy, wealthy, and wise, only one is going to get you a good seat at a restaurant. Now that everyone has finally sold out for a life of materialist depravity, it is time to face some hard economic facts. The free marketplace has seen us coming. Prices are pure sadism, and no one knows the safe word. We've become a nation of MBAs with hot plates and a standard of living you can't dress up and take anywhere. But there is something you should know before heading back to the commune you glossed over on your résumé. To keep things honest through the coming bad years, the issuers of money, checks, and credit cards are keeping secrets from us. Take a five-dollar bill out of your wallet and look carefully at the back. . . .

6·

Weird Stuff on Money

The Five-Dollar Bill

The U.S. Treasury Department denies that there are any secret anticounterfeiting gimmicks in currency artwork. Many people think otherwise. For some reason, the most popular hunting ground for anticounterfeiting devices—or clues to some unspecified conspiracy—is the picture of the Lincoln Memorial on the back of the five-dollar bill.

For instance, there's the "secret number." Look in the bushes to the left of the steps leading up to the Memorial. The pattern of shading seems to spell out a three-digit number: 372. The numerals are dark against a lighter background. The 3 has an exaggerated lower stroke; the 7 has a strong downward serif at the left end of the horizontal stroke. The shadows in the bushes on the right form no coherent pattern.

Once you see the 372, it's hard not to see it. Persistent rumors allege that the number must have some significance—but stop short of explaining just what purpose a barely legible, unchanging three-digit number could serve. The number is too coarse to be a useful anticounterfeiting device. A counterfeit bill so grainy as to smear the secret number would certainly have a funny-looking Lincoln on the other side. The Treasury Department doggedly maintains the number is a mere accident of engraving.

No accident are the near-invisible names of twenty-six U.S. states in the same engraving. Sucker bet: Get someone to wager five dollars that North Dakota is not mentioned on U.S. currency. You will need a magnifying glass to collect.

The state names are in two rows. The larger, bottom row of names is on the frieze above the tops of the twelve columns. Directly above each column is a roundish ornament suggesting two intersecting circles. These ornaments separate the eleven state names in this row. From left to right the names read (in order of admission to the union): DELAWARE PENNSYLVANIA NEW JERSEY GEORGIA CONNECTICUT MASSACHU-SETTS MARYLAND CAROLINA HAMPSHIRE VIR-GINIA NEW YORK. Each letter is less than half a millimeter high. With good lighting and a fresh bill, persons of excellent eyesight can just read the names. The outlines of the letters are incomplete because of the small scale.

An even finer row of fifteen states appears on the frieze on the upper, indented part of the Memorial. These names are on the lower, less ornamented section of the upper part, just below the smooth horizontal molding. They read: ARKANSAS MICHIGAN FLORIDA TEXAS IOWA WISCONSIN CALIFORNIA MINNESOTA OREGON KANSAS WEST VIRGINIA NEVADA NEBRASKA COLORADO NORTH DAKOTA. These names are virtually impossible to read unless you use a magnifying glass and follow the list. Depending on bill wear, some states may be illegible even with magnification.

The names appear on the Lincoln Memorial in Washington; any detailed picture of the Memorial must contain them. It is not clear if the engraver realized that they could be used as a check against counterfeiting. Because the names are almost invisible on a legitimate bill, they aren't likely to show up well on a photographically reproduced counterfeit. Of course, the checker must realize how faint the names can be on a real bill.

Still another object of suspicion is the funny shadow on the Memorial steps. It draws attention even though it could hardly serve any anticounterfeiting purpose. The peculiar shadow—that of the left stair guard and its torchlike ornament—seems to be much longer than it should be. The angle of sunlight can be judged from the shadow of the top of the Memorial, behind the leftmost columns. If a line parallel to this line of shadow is drawn from the top of the bowl or torch on the left stair guard, it intersects the steps much closer than the far end of the engraved shadow. Furthermore, the right stair guard doesn't cast any shadow on the bushes. Geometrically correct or not, the shadow would be easily duplicated in any counterfeiting process.

What do Treasury agents really look for on a suspected counterfeit? Most published sources say the eyes of the portrait are the best places to look. The eyes may not be any more susceptible to poor printing, but the right portion of the brain is quick to pick up on any slight modification in a familiar face. Another trick uses a hair-thin line that appears on the front but not the back of the five-dollar bill. (It is also on the front and back of one-, ten-, and twenty-dollar bills.)

Look at the large 5s in the upper right and upper left corners of the front of the five-dollar bill. Just inside the margin of the 5s is a fine dark line. Normally the line is sharp and entire. The fineness of the line makes it difficult to reproduce. It almost always comes out with parts of the line faded or missing. This scarcely changes the basic look of the bill, but if you know the line should be entire, it is a simple check. A faded line on a bill that otherwise seems unworn is particularly suspicious.

The One-Dollar Bill

The remarkable part of the one-dollar bill is the Great Seal of the United States (the two circular emblems on the back). Some see in the seal evidence of a Masonic conspiracy. At any rate, the pyramid with the eye above it is an obvious nod to Freemasonry. (The truncated pyramid represents the unfinished Temple of Solomon; the eye represents the Grand Architect of the Universe.)

In 1954 University of Texas doctoral candidate James David Carter wrote a dissertation (*Freemasonry in Texas: Background, History, and Influence to 1846*) that summarized further rumored significance of the Great Seal. It is claimed that the eagle on the seal has thirty-two feathers in its right wing and thirty-three feathers in its left. The thirty-two feathers symbolize the thirty-two Scottish Rite degrees (earned titles) of Freemasonry. There is also a thirty-third honorary degree, which accounts for the thirty-three feathers. The eagle's nine tail feathers correspond to the nine degrees of the York Rite. "E Pluribus Unum," on the eagle's banner, is a Masonic motto. Above the eagle's head are thirteen stars, representing the thirteen colonies but arranged to suggest a Star of David. King David figures into Masonic legend. The glory around the thirteen stars is calibrated with alternating long and short marks, suggesting the twenty-four divisions of the Masonic gauge (ruler).

Not all these claims check out. The thirty-third feather is elusive. There are three rows of feathers on each wing. The outer row on each wing has seventeen feathers. The middle row seems to have fifteen feathers on each wing. Together, that makes thirty-two feathers for each wing. The feathers in the inner row are lighter and hard to count. There seem to be about twelve inner feathers on each wing, which would not help achieve thirty-three in any case.

There are indeed nine tail feathers, and the stars do form a Star of David. But there are twenty-eight, not twenty-four, divisions of the glory.

Another Masonic symbol of sorts is on the front of the one-dollar bill. George Washington was a Mason and is venerated by American lodges—as are fellow Masons (and Presidents) Monroe, Jackson, Polk, Buchanan, Andrew Johnson, Garfield, McKinley, both Roosevelts, Taft, Harding, Truman, and Ford.

Other People's Money

U.S. greenbacks are a cinch to counterfeit compared to many foreign currencies. Not only do foreign currencies carry watermarks (a valuable anticounterfeiting device the U.S. Treasury has declined to use), but they also sport various high-tech gimmicks.

Buried inside the Scottish pound note is a strip of microfilm. Across the top of the front of the one-pound note is written "The Royal Bank of Scotland Limited." The microfilm runs vertically through the "n" in the word "Bank." If you hold the note up to a light and examine the strip with a magnifying glass, the film is seen to spell out the initials of the Royal Bank of Scotland: RBS.

Israeli currency has an opaque magnetic filament that is said to spell out the name of the central bank magnetically, in Morse code.

The Day-Glo colors on many Third World currencies are there for a reason. Bahamian money, for instance, has a "prismatic background"—a delicate pattern of conch shells that grades from turquoise to lilac to pink to orange to gold. A counterfeiter trying to reproduce the pastel tones on a color copier runs into trouble. Fiddle with the color adjustments as he might, at least one of the colors fails to reproduce.

Queen Elizabeth II's hair has been a source of notaphilic

rumors in the Commonwealth nations. The 1954 issue of Canadian dollars contained a remarkably convincing devil's face in the Queen's hair, just to the right of her earring. The portrait was retouched after public discovery of the face. Now the devil's-face dollars are virtually uncirculated (collectors hoard them). The face was claimed to have been the work of an antiroyalist engraver. The current portrait of the Queen on British pound notes has what may be interpreted as a panting Pekinese dog. It is also in the hair, on the right side, directly in line with the Queen's eyes.

7.

Currency Paper

The Treasury Department does not produce the paper used to print money. The paper's manufacture is contracted out to a private company better known for business stationery: Crane and Company of Dalton, Massachusetts. The type of currency paper now used, with the red and blue fibers, was developed by the Treasury Department in conjunction with Crane and Company. It has been in use since 1879.

Officially, the formulation of the paper is a secret. In fact, however, there is very little that isn't known about the paper. Every counterfeiter since 1879 has tried to duplicate it, with varying degrees of success. From time to time, curious paper chemists have broken it down and surmised its salient features. It's known, for instance, that the paper is 75 percent cotton and 25 percent linen. (Originally it was 100 percent linen, then 75 percent, and then 50 percent.) It is permeated with red and blue fibers. U.S. currency has three hidden security features:

1. The paper fluoresces under an ultraviolet lamp.
2. The ink is magnetic—not to a degree you could notice with a pocket magnet, but enough to be detected with special machines.
3. The paper is riddled with tiny, invisible holes. Under a microscope, pinpoints of light shine through. (Many counterfeit papers are solid.)

Money used to be made from used clothing. Crane purchased old cotton shirts, hired ragpickers to remove the buttons, and bleached the fabric white. Now most shirts contain polyester, and the dyes don't bleach out. "New rag cuttings"—small squares of virgin fabric—rather than old shirts are the principal raw material of money today. Crane buys them from textile firms.

The first step in the production of any rag paper is to convert the rag into pulp. The cuttings of cotton and linen (in a three-to-one ratio) are mixed with water—probably just about enough to cover the cloth—and beaten in large machines. Hours later, the mixture is a uniform pulp with no fibers remaining.

The blue and red fibers must be added at this stage. If they were added during the beating, the colored fibers would likewise be reduced to pulp. Examination of the finished currency paper reveals that the fibers are embedded in the paper, not just pasted onto its surface. Therefore they must be mixed into the pulp before the sheets are formed.

The pulp is poured into molds. Paper molds usually consist of a wooden frame with a fine wire mesh bottom. They are somewhat larger than the dry, finished sheets to allow for shrinkage. The pulp must be spread evenly in the mold, and the amount of pulp must be gauged to a final dry-sheet thickness in the range of 0.0042 to 0.0045 inch.

Excess water drips through the wire mesh, leaving a newly formed sheet in the mold. The damp sheets are probably "couched" as most fine paper is—carefully transferred to wool mats or "felts." The sheets and felts are sandwiched together and squeezed in a press to remove further water.

The next step is loft drying, to which currency paper owes much of its durability. The sheets are peeled from the felts and placed on a large screen, the loft, to dry. The faster paper dries, the stronger it becomes; the loft allows it to dry from both sides at once.

Paper to be used for printing must be "sized." Sizing prevents the ink from soaking in and spreading out. If you tried to write on a paper towel (an unsized paper) with a fountain pen, the ink would feather and the writing become illegible. Currency paper, then, obviously is well sized to take the fine engraving. The best sizing material, and the one that paper chemists agree is used for

U.S. currency, is glue. Glue sizing is actually a gelatin made by boiling the hoofs, ears, and other unused parts of slaughtered livestock. It is sold in a dry, flaky form and dissolved in water to yield a thin sizing bath. Dry sheets are immersed in the bath, removed, pressed, and dried.

The exceptional uniformity of currency paper betrays the final step in its manufacture. No matter how carefully the pulp is spread in the molds, even thickness is impossible to ensure without plate finishing. In this step the sheets are sandwiched between polished metal plates. Heavy rollers compress the sandwiched sheets under great pressure. Although mere lagniappe, this finishing is nearly impossible to duplicate with makeshift equipment. High-pressure rollers are expensive machines. (In contrast, all the steps up to plate finishing can be duplicated by amateur papermakers at home.) The thickness of counterfeit paper usually varies outside the Treasury Department tolerances.

The finished sheets are cut to measure 53.5 by 63.0 centimeters—just enough for thirty-two bills, eight down and four across.

8.

Credit Cards

There are at least three types of security devices on credit cards that you aren't supposed to know about. They are the account number, the signature panel, and the magnetic strip.

The Account Number

A Social Security card has nine digits. So do two-part Zip codes. A domestic phone number, including area code, has ten digits. Yet a complete MasterCard number has twenty digits. Why so many?

It is not mathematically necessary for any credit-card account number to have more than eight digits. Each cardholder must, of course, have a unique number. Visa and MasterCard are estimated to have about sixty-five million cardholders each. Thus their numbering systems must have at least sixty-five million available numbers.

There are one hundred million possible combinations of eight digits—00000000, 00000001, 00000002, 00000003, all the way up to 99999999. So eight digits would be enough. To allow for future growth, an issuer the size of Visa or MasterCard could opt for nine digits—enough for a billion different numbers.

In fact, a Visa card has thirteen digits and sometimes more. An American Express card has fifteen digits. Diners Club cards have fourteen. Carte Blanche has ten. Obviously, the card issuers are not projecting that they will have billions and billions of cardholders and need those digits to ensure a different number for each. The extra digits are actually a security device.

Say your Visa number is 4211 503 417 268. Each purchase must be entered into a computer from a sales slip. The account number tags the purchase to your account. The persons who enter account numbers into computers get bored and sometimes make mistakes. They might enter 4211 503 471 268 or 4211 703 417 268 instead.

The advantage of the thirteen-digit numbering system is that it is unlikely any Visa cardholder has 4211 503 471 268 or 4211 703 417 268 for an account number. There are 10 trillion possible thirteen-digit Visa numbers (0000 000 000 000; 0000 000 000 001; . . . 9999 999 999 999). Only about sixty-five million of those numbers are numbers of actual, active accounts. The odds that an incorrectly entered number would correspond to a real number are something like sixty-five million in ten trillion, or about one in one hundred fifty thousand.

Those are slim odds. You could fill up a book the size of this one with random thirteen-digit numbers such as these:

3901	160	943	791
1090	734	231	410
1783	205	995	561
9542	425	195	969
2358	862	307	845
9940	880	814	778
8421	456	150	662
9910	441	036	483
3167	186	869	267
6081	132	670	781
1228	190	300	350
4563	351	105	207

Still you would not duplicate a Visa account number. Whenever an account number is entered incorrectly, it will almost certainly fail to match up with any of the other account numbers in the computer's memory. The computer can then request that the number be entered again.

Other card-numbering systems are even more secure. Of the quadrillion possible fifteen-digit American Express card numbers, only about 11 million are assigned. The chance of a random number happening to correspond to an existing account number is about one in ninety million. Taking into account all twenty digits on a MasterCard, there are one hundred quintillion (100,000,000,000,000,000,000) possible numbers for sixty-five million cardholders. The chance of a random string of digits matching a real MasterCard number is about one in one and a half trillion.

Among other things, this makes possible those television ads inviting holders of credit cards to phone in to order merchandise. The operators who take the calls never see the callers' cards nor their signatures. How can they be sure the callers even have credit cards?

They base their confidence on the security of the credit-card numbering systems. If someone calls in and makes up a credit-card number—even being careful to get the right number of digits—the number surely will not be an existing real credit-card number. The deception can be spotted instantly by plugging into the credit-card company's computers. For all practical purposes, the only way to come up with a genuine credit-card number is to read it off a credit card. The number, not the piece of plastic, is enough.

Neiman-Marcus' Garbage Can

The converse of this is the fact that anyone who knows someone else's card number can charge to that person's account. Police sources say this is a major problem, but card issuers, by and large, do their best to keep these crimes a secret. The fear is that publicizing the crimes may tempt more people to commit them. Worse yet, there is almost nothing the average person can do to prevent being victimized—short of giving up credit cards entirely.

Lots of strangers know your credit-card numbers. Everyone you hand a card to—waiters, sales clerks, ticket agents, hairdressers, gas station attendants, hotel cashiers—sees the account number. Every time a card is put in an imprinter, three copies are made, and two are left with the clerk. If you charge anything by phone or mail order, someone somewhere sees the number.

Crooks don't have to be in a job with normal access to credit-card numbers. Occasional operations have discovered that the garbage cans outside prestige department or specialty stores are sources of high-credit-limit account numbers. The crooks look for the discarded carbon paper from sales slips. The account number is usually legible—as are the expiration date, name, and signature. (A 1981 operation used carbons from Koontz Hardware, a West Hollywood, California, store frequented by many celebrities.)

Converting a number into cash is less risky than using a stolen credit card. The crook need only call an airline, posing as the cardholder, and make a reservation on a heavily traveled flight. He usually requests that tickets be issued in someone else's name for pickup at the airport. The someone else is an accomplice or an identity for which he has bogus ID. Crook or accomplice picks up the tickets at the airport (airlines don't always ask for ID on ticket pickups, but the crook has it if needed) and is set. The tickets can be sold at a discount on the hot-ticket market operating in every major airport.

There are other methods as well. Anyone with a Visa or MasterCard merchant account can fill out invoices for nonexistent sales and submit them to the bank. As long as the account numbers and names are genuine, the bank will pay the merchant immediately.

For an investment of about a thousand dollars, an organized criminal operation can get the pressing machines needed to make counterfeit credit cards. Counterfeiting credit cards is relatively simple. There are no fancy scrolls and filigree work, just blocky logos in primary colors. From the criminal's standpoint, the main advantage of a counterfeit card is that it allows him to get cash advances. For maximum plundering of a line of credit, the crook must know the credit limit as well as the account number. To learn both, he often calls an intended victim, posing as the victim's bank:

> CROOK: This is Bank of America. We're calling to tell you that the credit limit on your Visa card has been raised to twelve hundred dollars.
> VICTIM: But my limit has always been ten thousand dollars.
> CROOK: There must be some problem with the computers. Do you have your card handy? Could you read off the embossed number?

On a smaller scale, many struggling rock groups have discovered the knack of using someone else's telephone company credit card. When a cardholder wants to make a long-distance call from a hotel or pay phone, he or she reads the card number to the operator. The call is then billed to the cardholder's home phone. Musicians on tour sometimes wait by the special credit-card-and-collect-calls-only booths at airports and jot down a few credit-card numbers. In this way unsuspecting businesspeople finance a touring act's calls to friends at home. If the musicians call from public phones, use a given card number only once, and don't stay in one city long, the phone company seems helpless to stop them.

What makes all of these scams so hard to combat is the lead time afforded the criminal. Theft of a credit card—a crime that card issuers will talk about—is generally reported immediately. Within twenty-four hours, a stolen card's number is on the issuer's "hot list" and can no longer be used. But when only a card number is being used illicitly, the crime is not discovered until the cardholder receives his first inflated bill. That's at least two weeks later; it could be as much as six weeks later. As long as the illicit user isn't too greedy, he has at least two weeks to tap into a credit line with little risk.

The Signature Panel

You're not supposed to erase the signature panel, of course. Card issuers fear that crooks might erase the signature on a stolen credit card and replace it with their own. To make alteration more difficult, many card signature panels have a background design that rubs off if anyone tries to erase. There's the "fingerprint" design on the American Express panel, repeated Visa or MasterCard logos on some bank cards, and the "Safesig" design on others. The principle is the same as with the security paper used for checks. If you try to erase a check on security paper, the wavy-line pattern erases, leaving a white area—and it is obvious that the check has been altered.

Rumors hint of a more elaborate gimmick in credit-card panels. It is said that if you erase the panel, a secret word—VOID—appears to prevent use of the card. To test this rumor, fifteen common credit cards were sacrificed.

An ordinary pen eraser will erase credit-card signature panels, if slowly. The panels are more easily removed with a cloth and a dry-cleaning fluid such as Energine. This method dissolves the panels cleanly. Of the fifteen cards tested, six had nothing under the panel (other than a continuation of the card back design, where there was one). Nine cards had the word "VOID" under the panel. In all cases, the VOIDs were printed small and repeated many times under the panel. The breakdown:

VOID Device	*Nothing*
Bloomingdale's	American Express Gold Card
Bonwit Teller	Broadway
Bullock's	MasterCard (Citibank)
Chase Convenience	Neiman-Marcus
Banking Card	Robinson's
First Interstate Bank Card	Saks Fifth Avenue
I. Magnin	
Joseph Magnin	
Montgomery Ward	
Visa (Chase Manhattan)	

When held to a strong light, the VOIDs were visible through the Bloomingdale's card even without removing the panel.

The VOID device isn't foolproof. Any criminal who learns the secret will simply refrain from trying to erase the signature. Most salesclerks don't bother to check signatures anyway.

Moreover, it is possible to paint the signature panel back in, over the VOIDs—at least on those cards that do not have a design on the panel. (Saks' panel is a greenish-tan khaki color that would be difficult to match with paint.) The panel is first removed with dry-cleaning fluid. The back of the card is covered with masking tape, leaving a window where the replacement panel is to go. A thin coat of flat white spray paint simulates the original panel.

The Magnetic Strip

The other security device on the back of the card, the brown magnetic strip, is more difficult to analyze. Some people think there are sundry personal details about the cardholder stored in the strip. But the strip has no more information capacity than a similar snippet of recording tape. For their part, banks are reticent about the strip.

The strip need not contain any information other than the account number or similar indentification. Any further information needed to complete an automatic-teller transaction—such as current account balances—can be called up from bank computers and need not be encoded in the strip.

Evidently, the card expiration date is in the strip. Expired cards are "eaten" by automatic-teller machines even when the expired card has the same account number and name as its valid replacement card. Credit limit, address, phone number, employer, etc., must not be indicated in the strip, for banks do not issue new cards just because this information changes.

It is not clear if the personal identification number is in the strip or called up from the bank computer. Many automatic-teller machines have a secret limit of three attempts for providing the correct personal identification number. After three wrong attempts, the "customer" is assumed to be a crook with a stolen card, going through all the possible permutations—and the card is eaten.

It is possible to scramble the information in the strip by rubbing a pocket magnet over it. Workers in hospitals or research facilities with large electromagnets sometimes find that their cards no longer work in automatic-teller machines. (If you try to use a magnetically doctored card, you usually get a message to the effect, "Your card may be inserted incorrectly. Please remove and insert according to diagram.")

The Bloomingdale's Color Code

Only in a few cases does the color of a credit card mean anything. There are, of course, the American Express, Visa, and Master-Card gold cards for preferred customers. The Air Travel Card comes in red and green, of which green is better. (With red, you can charge tickets for travel within North America only.) The most elaborate color scheme, and a source of some confusion to status-conscious queues, is that of Bloomingdale's credit cards. The five colors of Bloomingdale's cards do not signify credit limits per se, but they do tip off the sales staff as to what type of customer you are. According to Bloomingdale's credit department, here is how it works: Low color in the pecking order is blue, issued to Bloomingdale's employees as a perk in their compensation packages. The basic Bloomie's card is yellow. Like most department store cards, it can be used to spread payments over several months with the payment of a finance charge. The red card gives holders three months' free interest and is issued to customers who regularly make large purchases. The silver card is good for unlimited spending, but as with a travel and entertainment card, all charges must be paid in thirty days. The gold card offers the same payment options as the yellow card but is reserved for the store's biggest spenders.

9·

The VOID Pop-up

What happens if you photocopy something you're not supposed to photocopy? If it is a finely engraved document—money, a traveler's check, a stock certificate—the copy comes out smudged or faded. If it is a simpler document—a money order, a supermarket coupon, a gift certificate—and if you use a good color copier, the copy is often a convincing counterfeit.

The VOID pop-up is a secret gimmick to foil the latter type of counterfeiters. It works simply enough: When a document containing the device is photocopied, the word "VOID" appears on the copy. At best the VOID is faint and fuzzy, like the Shroud of Turin. But users of the pop-up feel it must take a lot more guts to try to pass a counterfeit with the VOID than without it.

The VOID pop-up was invented by the American Bank Note Company but not patented. It has been adopted by other document printers. It is not regarded as effective a security device as currency-quality engraving. The time and expense of engraving make it suitable only for the most important documents, however. The VOID pop-up has been used mostly for medium-security documents, including, according to American Bank Note, Chase Manhattan Bank money orders and Kentucky Fried Chicken gift certificates.

The VOID pop-up uses a screen—a background of dots so fine they appear as an even gray or pastel shade. From a normal viewing distance, the only distinguishing feature of a screen is how dark a gray it is (assuming black dots on a white background; the same argument applies for other ink colors). In turn, the shade of gray depends only on the percentage of the total area that is covered by the dots.

Two different screens can look the same. One screen might have larger dots, a different arrangement of dots, or a different shape from another. But as long as the percentage of black area to white area is the same, and as long as the individual dots are too small to be seen individually, both screens look the same shade of gray.

Two such different but seemingly identical screens can make a VOID pop up. One screen is used to print the letters VOID across the document. The other screen forms a background to the letters. Both screens have exactly the same density, so the original document seems to have an even gray or pastel background.

A Xerox machine sees things differently from the eye. One of the screens is chosen so that the configuration of its dots will bleed together on the copy. This screen comes out darker or of a different quality than the other, and the VOID is visible.

The system isn't foolproof. Copiers vary, so the VOID is conspicuous with some machines, scarcely noticeable with others. Occasionally a ghostly VOID is visible on the original, to the consternation of innocent consumers who aren't intended to know about the pop-up at all. There is a screen attachment for some makes of copiers that defeats the pop-up and allows clean copies.

There are still other ways to prevent illicit photocopying. *Prospects/New Book News,* a New York-based weekly newsletter that summarizes the plots of upcoming novels for motion-picture producers, is printed on red paper. Red shows up nearly black on most black-and-white copiers. (As subscriptions are five hundred dollars a year, producers are sorely tempted to make Xerox copies for associates.) Of course, *Prospects* can be copied on a color copier, and on those black-and-white machines that have red filters.

At the other end of the spectrum, a light, swimming-pool-bottom blue does not reproduce on most copiers. Turquoise felt-tip pens are used to make marginal notes on magazine boards. The notes are invisible in the photographically printed magazines. In 1971 *Computerworld,* a trade publication, postulated the following use of light-blue print:

> The Diners Club, whose accounting system has been at-
> tacked by people trying to keep their accounts straight, has

apparently found one way of keeping the complaint level down—particularly those types of complaints that are copied to various federal and state authorities, Better Business Bureaus, Ralph Nader, etc. It won't, of course stop the complaints altogether, but it will certainly reduce their effectiveness in many cases.

What Diners Club did was redesign the forms, printing much of the vital data in non-reproducing blue. As a result, after it has been put into the copying machine, the output simply is almost incomprehensible, and certainly much less persuasive to other people who may want to read it.

According to Diners Club, the color choice was a coincidence—the Diners Club logo is blue.

10·

The Universal Product Code

Supermarkets know better than to trust us anarchists. It is easy enough to take a magic marker and black out a line or two of the Universal Product Code symbol. Lest anyone try to lower prices or sabotage the system, there is a security device built into the code.

The UPC scanner can detect any alteration of a symbol—or, at least, stands a 90 percent chance of detecting it. The secret is a "check digit" encoded in two extra bars at the end of the UPC symbol. The check digit is derived mathematically from the information contained in the other bars of the symbol. Change the symbol, and the check digit probably no longer jibes.

The formula for assigning the check digit was devised by the Uniform Product Code Council, a manufacturers' association based in Dayton, Ohio. It is revealed in *The UPC Guidelines Manual,* a technical bulletin provided to corporate members of the council. Every manufacturer using the Universal Product Code calculates the check digit in the same way.

In its usual form, the code symbol has a number at the left side of the bar pattern and two groups of five digits at the bottom of the bar pattern. A shorter form of the symbol, with only six digits at the bottom, is used on packages too small to take the full symbol. A few products, such as magazines and books, have extra numbers and bars to accommodate large numbers of products from a single manufacturer.

The scanners do not read the numerals. The numerals are there

How to Crack the Universal Product Code

A Two thin "guard bars" don't mean anything; they frame the real message. Repeated in middle and at other end of bar pattern.

B Wide space, bar, narrow space, thin bar encode the 0 at left of symbol. 0 means it's regular groceries. 3 is for drugs.

C Ten spaces and ten bars encode the 12345 at bottom, which identifies the manufacturer. 21000 would be Kraft, etc.

D Encodes the 67890, which identifies the product, including size of package. Price is not encoded.

E A secret "check digit" (here 5) to catch any error or tampering. If someone widens a bar with a felt-tip pen, the check digit helps the scanner detect it.

only for the convenience of the human checkers. If the scanner is down, the checker may enter the numbers by hand. The bars encode the same set of numbers—plus the check digit—in a form that can be read by machine. The check digit is always a whole number from 0 to 9. It is not usually printed in numeral form. (On the few packages where the check digit is printed out, it is smaller than the other digits and appears below the two bars that encode it.)

The other digits of the code are assigned simply enough. The lone digit to the left of the bar pattern is the "number system character." A "0" means the item is an ordinary grocery item; "2" is used for variable-weight items, such as meat and produce; "3" is for drugs and health-related items; "5" is for cents-off coupons.

The first cluster of five digits at the bottom encodes the manufacturer. For instance, 43000 is General Foods; 37000 is Procter & Gamble; 11141 is A&P house brand; 51000 is Campbell Soup. The second cluster of five digits specifies the product and size of package. These five digits are assigned by the manufacturers individually. If 20043 means a ten-ounce can of tomato soup for one manufacturer, it needn't mean tomato soup for another manufacturer.

Once a product is encoded as a number, the next step is to encode the number in a bar pattern. The bar pattern can vary in size; 0.816 inch by 1.175 inches is the minimum; 2.040 inches by 2.938 inches is the maximum. The dark bars may be almost any dark color (not red). The background may be white or pastel.

The first two bars, reading from left to right, signify nothing. They are a sort of punctuation to let the scanner know where to start reading. The same is true for the two bars in the middle, which extend down between the two clusters of visible digits, and for the two bars at the extreme right.

The first two bars to the right of the first set of punctuation bars encode the number system character, the visible digit at left center. If this digit is a zero, there is a space, then a thick bar, then a narrow space, then a narrow bar: the bar code for zero.

Each of the other digits also appears as two bars and two spaces. The portion of the UPC symbol allotted to each digit is composed of seven equal units or "modules," each of which may be either dark or light. The symbol for zero is three light modules (the space), two dark modules (the thick bar), one light module (the narrow space), and one dark module (the narrow bar). This is represented as 0001101, where the 0s are light modules and the 1s are dark modules.

A reversed version of this code is used for the part of the UPC symbol to the right of the two thin bars in the center. A zero appearing on the right becomes 1110010—that is, a thick bar, a space, a narrow bar, a narrow space. Two different codes are used so that the scanner will be able to recognize which side of the symbol it is reading. In this way, packages do not have to be fed to the scanner in one direction only.

The complete code is:

Digit	Left Side of Symbol	Right Side of Symbol
0	0001101	1110010
1	0011001	1100110
2	0010011	1101100
3	0111101	1000010
4	0100011	1011100
5	0110001	1001110
6	0101111	1010000
7	0111011	1000100
8	0110111	1001000
9	0001011	1110100

The check digit, appearing at the far right, is encoded according to the right-side column above. Two narrow bars separated by a triple-wide space signifies a 7, for instance.

Some typical codes, along with their check digits, are as follows:

Ann Page Black Pepper, 2 oz.	0 11141 26230 1
Ronzoni Spinach Fettuccine, 12 oz.	0 71300 00137 0
Campbell's Spanish Style Vegetable Soup, 10½ oz.	0 51000 02677 4

The formula? Take the digits of the code (aside from the check digit, of course) and group them according to their sequence in the code. Write the first digit, third digit, fifth digit, etc.—the odd sequence—on one line and the second digit, fourth digit, etc.—the even sequence—below it:

0 11141 26230 $\longrightarrow$ 0 1 4 2 2 0

1 1 1 6 3

Then add each sequence of digits,

$$0 + 1 + 4 + 2 + 2 + 0 = 9$$
$$1 + 1 + 1 + 6 + 3 = 12$$

multiply the sum of the odd sequence by 3,

$$9 \times 3 = 27$$

and add the result to the sum of the even sequence,

$$27 + 12 = 39$$

Subtract this result from the next higher multiple of 10. Here 40 is the next higher multiple of 10:

$$40 - 39 = 1$$

The remainder, 1, is the correct check digit.

Changing any single digit of the code will require a different check digit. In no case could a person with a marking pen expect to change a code to that of a lower-priced item; the best one could do would be to change a code randomly. Perhaps the altered code would be a cheaper item; perhaps it would be more expensive; perhaps it would be an unassigned code. The check digit ensures that any simple alteration will be caught, even if the altered code is an assigned one.

PART THREE

Kids, Don't Try This at Home

Dad's out working, Mom's out networking, and little Elroy and Judy are up to no good. Today's latchkey kids know what puts the "super" in "unsupervised." It's putting Sea Monkeys in the microwave to see if they explode. It's going to the 7-11 and inhaling the nitrous oxide propellant out of Reddi-Wip cans. It's playing William Wegman to the cat's Man Ray. It's drinking mouthwash for the alcohol, it's eating toothpaste to induce vomiting, it's fear and loathing with Procter & Gamble. The kids are *never* all right. And the real consumer education doesn't begin until the role models leave the house. Here are the secret lives of some of our pop consumables.

11·

Perfumes

Nearly all commercial perfume formulations are secret. A typical heavily merchandised fragrance—Chanel No. 5, Bal à Versailles, Joy—is a blend of many scents. Industry conviction is that a perfume that simulates a single, identifiable scent, such as rose or orange blossom, is difficult to market: Consumers assume a complex scent is better. Prospective customers are less likely to reject a scent if they can't explain why they don't like it. Instead of saying, "No, that smells like lily of the valley, and I don't like lily of the valley," they say, "Maybe." Or so the industry postulates.

Blending perfumes is a complex business. Good perfumers command salaries commensurate with those of investment bankers. It often takes years to formulate a fragrance. Some perfumes are reputed to contain as many as three hundred ingredients. Insiders say the large perfume houses routinely analyze each new competing fragrance as it is introduced. The analytic powers of "noses"—skilled perfume blenders—are legendary but have limits. Increasingly, gas chromatography and kindred techniques are used for analysis. Any sufficiently popular new fragrance is soon copied by competing manufacturers and sold under a different name. Thus Estée Lauder's Cinnabar, a cinnamonlike Oriental-type fragrance, seems to have inspired Yves Saint Laurent's Opium.

Is There Bobcat Urine in Perfume?

Most controversial of the hundreds of ingredients used in perfumes are the animal products. All are expensive, all are unsavory in the raw state, and all impart delightful notes when blended properly. Four animal products are used. None is urine (not that what they are is any more appealing).

Ambergris is a wax- or pitchlike substance found floating in tropic seas. It was used for fragrance, flavor, and alleged aphrodisiac properties long before anyone knew what it is. At various times, ambergris was held to be a gum; a bitumen; sea foam mysteriously solidified; the caked excrement of seabirds; a marine fungus; or honeycombs fallen into the sea from cliffside hives. Ambergris is now known to come from the sperm whale. The whale eats squid, and squid have sharp, indigestible "beaks." Ambergris is a secretion produced when the beaks irritate the wall of the whale's intestine. Squid beaks are often found in lumps of ambergris. It is not certain if the ambergris normally passes through the digestive tract or remains in the whale until death (lumps as large as 336 pounds have been reported.) Whaling ships occasionally take ambergris from fresh kills. Then the ambergris is black, tarry, and evil-smelling. Aged ambergris found in the ocean or on beaches may be hard, translucent, and white, gray, yellow, reddish, or striped. At best the odor is sweet, earthy, and lingering—a quality perfumers call "velvetiness."

Civet is a thick, yellowish secretion of anal glands of the civet cat of Asia and Africa. It figures in several confused stories about Chanel No. 5. Civet (or bobcat urine in some variations) is said to be an ingredient of Chanel No. 5. Some cat owners boycott Chanel perfume on the grounds that the animals are tortured. The civet cat is not really in the cat family, but it is a mammal capable of feeling discomfort. The secretion is produced by glands comparable to those that produce the scent in a skunk, and it is collected regularly from living animals. The animals are alleged to produce more civet when closely penned or agitated. As the animals are raised by independent operators unaffiliated with the major perfume houses, the claims of mistreatment are plausible. Civet's odor is objectionably musky at full strength; but pleasant when diluted.

Musk is usually a hardened, granular secretion from the male musk deer of Asia. Musk comes in a pouch, which is cut off and sold. Musk costs about twelve thousand dollars a pound. Frequently the musk is emptied from the pouch, cut with cheaper substances, and replaced. Musk's fragrance is not as lingering as that of ambergris. But musk's odor is so penetrating that it cannot be washed off polished steel. Despite its high price, musk is such a concentrated scent that it is probably never much of a factor in the price of a bottle of perfume. Castoreum, the fourth animal product used in perfumery, is a similar secretion, from the beaver.

How widespread is the use of animal products? One industry observer consulted thought it was decreasing—not so much because of cost as because of animal-protection lobbies. Only free-floating ambergris, of all the animal products, does not involve some form of molestation. Three prominent perfume houses were queried about use of animal products. Estée Lauder responded that it uses castoreum, civet, and musk in its perfume. According to Lauder's spokesperson, ambergris is not used by U.S. firms because of the whale's endangered-species status. Chanel acknowledged the use of civet in Chanel No. 5, noting that "most, if not all, other manufacturers of fine fragrances" do the same. Jean Patou denied use of any animal products in its Joy perfume.

Of course, animal products are only a small part of the picture. Despite trade secrecy, most perfumers have rough ideas of the composition of the major competing perfumes. Fragrance trade journals and books detail representative formulas, including occasional outside analyses of name perfumes. *Big Secrets* canvassed perfumers and fragrance ingredient suppliers for their ideas about several well-known perfumes. What follows are educated guesses. If, as seems likely, some of the actual formulas include dozens of trace ingredients, none of the sources consulted could identify them with any confidence. Nor is it always possible to distinguish a good synthetic component from its natural counterpart. Fragrances are listed in order of increasing retail price as of late 1982.

Eau Sauvage
Christian Dior
$7 per ounce ($13 for a 1.9-ounce bottle)

Bergamot, an obscure citrus fruit, seems to dominate Eau Sauvage. Because most men's colognes imitate the original eau de cologne devised by Johann Maria Farina, it isn't hard to give half a dozen ingredients that are almost certain to be in the Eau Sauvage formula. Basically, colognes blend oils of citrus peels with oils of herbs from the mint family. Oils of bergamot, lemon, neroli, lavender, rosemary, and petitgrain are probably in Eau Sauvage.

The bergamot orange is a misshapen, greenish-rust variety of the bitter orange. The bergamot orange is not eaten, but the oil flavors some candy and prepared foods. Bergamot oil is a universal ingredient in cologne and, along with lemon oil, seems to be responsible for the sharp, refreshing character of Eau Sauvage.

Neroli oil is the distilled essence of bitter orange blossoms; petitgrain is distilled from the leaves and twigs of the same tree. The pine or forest note in Eau Sauvage is probably from rosemary, not pine. Rose oil figures in some cologne formulations. If it is in Eau Sauvage, it is only a bare trace.

Cologne's relative cheapness is due to its dilution. Typically, about 7 grams of essential oils are used per liter of finished product. The rest is alcohol, water, and in some cases orange flower water or rose water. Assuming Eau Sauvage is of typical cologne strength, the 1.9-fluid-ounce bottle contains a scarce 0.39 gram of essential oils. That's about eight drops.

Reputedly, the best colognes are made from potato alcohol. Many modern perfumers dispute the importance of potato alcohol—alcohol should be alcohol, regardless of source. Better colognes are distilled, with the neroli oil and additional alcohol added after distillation. One to six months' aging is often recommended in standard formulas. As one of the most expensive men's colognes, it is likely that Eau Sauvage undergoes aging before being marketed.

Is the greenish-straw color natural? Some cologne essential oil mixtures have an amber color not too different from Eau Sauvage's, but the color is lost upon dilution to final strength. Like the perfumes that follow, Eau Sauvage has had a dye job.

Chanel No. 5
Chanel
$120 per ounce

The big secret here is synthetics. Chanel No. 5 was the first successful perfume to exploit fully a group of chemicals called fatty aldehydes. Despite the unpromising name, fatty aldehydes have revolutionized perfumery. They are usually denoted by the number of carbon atoms they contain—C_{10}, for instance, or C_{12}. Each aldehyde has a distinctive odor that often suggests some natural fragrance. Believed to be in Chanel No. 5 are:

C_9—to chemists, *n*-nonylaldehyde—a liquid with a pleasant rose odor. Chemical formula: $CH_3(CH_2)_7CHO$.

C_{10}, or *n*-decylaldehyde, with a sweet odor unlike that of any natural flower. Chemical formula: $CH_3(CH_2)_8CHO$.

C_{11}, or *n*-undecylaldehyde, with a strong rose odor. Chemical formula: $CH_3(CH_2)_9CHO$.

C_{12}, of which two distinct forms may be used. Lauraldehyde $[CH_3(CH_2)_{10}CHO]$ is a solid with an unpleasant, greasy odor. Diluted, the odor is agreeable. Methyl nonylacetaldehyde $[CH_3(CH_2)_8CH(CH_3)CHO]$ suggests a mixture of orange blossoms and ambergris.

There may be a synthetic vanilla note from vanillin or from coumarin. A likely natural oil is ylang-ylang, produced from the sweet, powerfully scented blossoms of a tree of the same name grown in Madagascar and the West Indies. There seems to be a woody component to Chanel No. 5. This could come from sandalwood, a parasitic tree from the Orient, or vetivert, a grass with aromatic roots. A trace of citrus oil may be present. As mentioned, Chanel's animal note is from civet.

Missoni
Missoni
$150 per ounce

The Missonis know sweaters, not perfume. Not surprisingly, the Missoni fragrance is simply a workmanlike retread of an old standard—the chypre fragrance. Chypre is the generic name for a type of perfume that originated on the island of Cyprus (Chypre to the French) by the twelfth century. Chypre perfumes are heavy, woody/spicy scents. There is less of a flowery character than with most perfumes. Missoni is not the only chypre scent on the market—though it seems to be the most expensive and, one would hope, one of the best made. Aramis and Miss Dior are also chypre scents. Chypre is popular with both sexes.

The three indispensable components of the chypre scent are oakmoss, patchouli, and sandalwood. Vetivert oil is usually present. (Missoni admits to "patchouli, vetivert, and spice" in an ad.) Oakmoss is a lichen—a gray-green encrustation that grows on the bark of oak and plum trees in the Mediterranean region. It is collected, made into an extract, and sold to perfumers and soap-makers wanting a woodsy scent. Patchouli is a shrubby Indone-sian mint. Its fragrance suggests both mint and sandalwood. True sandalwood enters into perfumes as an essential oil produced largely in India.

Like other modern chypre perfumes, Missoni seems to have a slight citrus note, perhaps from bergamot. There may be traces of jasmine and rose (probably natural) and vanilla (probably syn-thetic). Nearly all chypre formulations contain synthetic musk—nonanimal substances such as "musk ambrette," "musk ketone," and "musk xylene," which simulate the character of musk.

Bal à Versailles
Jean Desprez
$158 per ounce

Once hailed as the world's most expensive perfume, Bal à Ver-sailles now undersells several of its competitors. There seems to be little argument as to the main components of Bal à Versailles' flo-ral bouquet. They are jasmine, ylang-ylang, patchouli, and va-nilla. Ylang-ylang oil is sold in two grades, "Ylang No. 1" and "Ylang No. 2." Presumably Jean Desprez springs for the better Ylang No. 1. But there is scarcely any difference between natural vanilla and synthetic vanillin, so even Bal à Versailles may con-tain the cheaper synthetic.

Bal à Versailles' scent is relatively easy to simulate. Many per-fume houses offer Bal à Versailles knock-offs. This is done with other perfumes, of course, but Bal à Versailles imitations are often particularly convincing. Some savvy shoppers are convinced that one of these reproductions—"Naudet No. 3," sold by Essential Products Co. of New York—is slightly *better* than the original. Naudet No. 3 sells for $16 per ounce.

Joy
Jean Patou
$175 per ounce (regular bottle) or $400 per ounce (Baccarat crystal bottle)

For a flavor of the perfume industry doubletalk on pricing, con-sider: For years, Patou has advertised its Joy perfume as the "costliest" fragrance in the world. Joy costs $175 per ounce. But Patou also makes 1000 perfume—and 1000 costs $245 an ounce. When challenged, Patou management is said to allow that 1000 is indeed more expensive but insist that Joy is still *costlier*. The distinction, at least in Patou's dictionary, seems to mean that the ingredients of Joy cost more than those of the more expensive 1000. In other words, the markup on 1000 is a lot more. Perhaps to justify its "costlier" ingredients, Patou also offers Joy in a Baccarat crystal bottle for $400.

Joy is nothing more nor less than a very well-made rose perfume. High-quality natural rose oil is undoubtedly the main fragrance ingredient. The other ingredients merely gild the lily—make Joy smell more like a rose ought to smell than a rose does. These ingredients may include bergamot oil, heliotropin (a synthetic suggesting evergreens), and jasmine.

Patou says Joy contains no animal products, so evidently an ambergris substitute is used. One of the most satisfactory is a resin obtained from the Mediterranean labdanum shrub. The sticky, fragrant resin coats the leaves. It is boiled off, extracted with a solvent, or, in the case of a Cyprus variety of the shrub, combed from the wool of sheep or goats that graze among the bushes. It smells like balsam.

The ingredient list on the following page is from a recipe for an imitation of Joy perfume in *A Formulary of Cosmetic Preparations* by Michael Ash and Irene Ash (New York: Chemical Publishing Co., 1977). That recipe suggests ambergris and musk; synthetics have been substituted here to conform with Patou policy.

1000
Jean Patou
$245 per ounce

Patou's ultrastatus scent, 1000, is less sweet-and-conventional. A strong leafy note suggests a mown lawn, growing plants, or the "weedy" nuances of a Cabernet Sauvignon. Floral notes are muted.

There's no grass in 1000. Perfumers create the mown-lawn effect with two substances, coumarin and linalool. Coumarin can be extracted from the tonka bean, the seed of a South American tree. Coumarin is toxic and not permitted as a flavoring in the

Joy Perfume: Ingredients—an Educated Guess

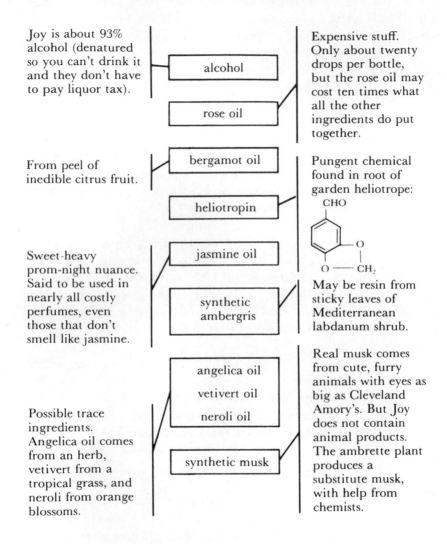

Joy is about 93% alcohol (denatured so you can't drink it and they don't have to pay liquor tax).

alcohol

rose oil

Expensive stuff. Only about twenty drops per bottle, but the rose oil may cost ten times what all the other ingredients do put together.

From peel of inedible citrus fruit.

bergamot oil

heliotropin

Pungent chemical found in root of garden heliotrope:

Sweet-heavy prom-night nuance. Said to be used in nearly all costly perfumes, even those that don't smell like jasmine.

jasmine oil

synthetic ambergris

May be resin from sticky leaves of Mediterranean labdanum shrub.

Possible trace ingredients. Angelica oil comes from an herb, vetivert from a tropical grass, and neroli from orange blossoms.

angelica oil

vetivert oil

neroli oil

synthetic musk

Real musk comes from cute, furry animals with eyes as big as Cleveland Amory's. But Joy does not contain animal products. The ambrette plant produces a substitute musk, with help from chemists.

United States, but it is used in perfumes. Coumarin's chemical formula is:

Linalool is present in bergamot oil. Its formula is:

$$CH_2{:}CHCOH(CH_3)CH_2CH_2CH{:}C(CH_3)_2$$

The floral background of 1000 seems to include natural rose and jasmine oils. Violet and tuberose—natural or artificial—may be present.

Are Perfumes Overpriced?

One of the reasons for all the secrecy is the cost. Once the ingredients of a perfume are known, the cost of raw materials can be estimated. In most cases, this cost is a small fraction of the retail sales price—a fact of life in the fragrance industry but one they'd prefer not to publicize.

This is not to say that perfume manufacturers are making a killing. The actual profit to manufacturer is a small part of the gaping difference between ingredient costs and sale price. Manufacturers of fragrances tied to a designer name pay a royalty to the designer (who rarely gives more than a name to the creation). There is often an under-the-table spiff paid to department store salespersons to push a perfume. Bottle and packaging are expensive (if not always to the tune of the $225 you pay for the Baccarat crystal bottle of Joy). Promotion and assorted overhead expenses make up the rest. A 1974 *New York Times* article drew industry ire for estimating these expenses for a then-costly $35 bottle of perfume. The *Times* analysis claimed the following breakdown (here converted from dollar amounts to percentages):

Fragrance oils, alcohol, and blending 13%

Bottle (crystal) and packaging 8%

Royalty for use of couturier or designer name
    (this arrangement varies considerably with
    different names) 3%

Advertising, sales promotion, sampling 11%

Commission paid to salesclerks in stores (usually
    4% to 10% of manufacturing costs) 4%
Administration and overhead 11%
Research, development, and quality control 1%
Taxes 4%
Net profit to manufacturer 4%
Store markup 40%
(Percentages do not total 100% because of rounding.)

Many perfume ingredients are fabulously expensive. The best floral essences can cost $2,000 a pound or more; musk costs about $12,000 a pound. But in most cases a little goes a long way.

Take the *Formulary of Cosmetic Preparations* recipe for imitation Joy. It is hard to say how closely it matches Jean Patou's formula for Joy. However, most perfumes are blended at roughly the same fragrance strength. Joy could hardly contain much more essential oil than specified in the imitation recipe. Moreover, the formulary recipe uses good, expensive ingredients. If the required amounts of ingredients are multiplied by the prices, the results are the ingredient costs—for the imitation Joy, at any rate.

The ingredient prices below are typical. Prices vary according to quality, amount purchased, and market fluctuations. Actual amounts of synthetic ambergris and musk might have to be juggled according to the strength of the substitutes.

Ingredient	Grams per Ounce of Perfume	Price per Pound	Price of Ingredient per Ounce of Perfume
Alcohol	26.3	$.50	$.029
Rose oil	1.06	2,000	4.67
Bergamot oil	0.548	22	.027
Heliotropin	0.274	8.75	.0053
Jasmine oil	0.109	1,500	.36
Synthetic ambergris	0.0547	100 (?)	.012
Angelica oil	0.000155	75	.000026
Vetivert oil	0.000155	50	.000017
Neroli oil	0.0000773	8.50	.000014
Synthetic musk	0.0000773	100 (?)	.000017

Only five ingredients contribute so much as a penny to the final per-ounce cost. The total per-ounce cost: about $5.15, most of it for rose oil.

12·

Playing Cards

1.   **2.**   **3.**   **4.**

1. *Bee:* Nevada casinos use it. Small, busy pattern, no margin. Favored for bottom-dealing.
2. *Aviator:* Does the white margin foil cheaters?
3. *Bicycle:* Popular with the Brach's Bridge Mix crowd but easy to mark—all those little birds, dots, flowers.
4. *United Airlines:* The savvy gambler's choice: more cheatproof than the commercial brands. And you can use the airsick bag to keep score.

It is not easy to design cheatproof playing cards, if possible at all. Most card manufacturers do not even try. Cheaters, however, are aware of the back design as a security device. With certain back designs, it is more difficult to bottom- or second-deal undetected than with other designs. Some backs are easier to mark than others.

For bottom- or second-dealing, the ideal deck would be one

with a solid-color back. With such a deck it would be hard for the other players to tell whether the top card is sliding forward and off the deck (as it should in a legal deal) or staying on top (as in a bottom- or second-deal).

None of the readily available brands of cards has a solid-color back. In practice, bottom-dealers favor brands with small, regular patterns—patterns that are just a blur of color in a brisk deal. Diamond-pattern Bee (back no. 67) and Club Reno are examples.

A white margin ruins a deck for bottom-dealing. As the bottom (or second) card is drawn out, the other players see its white margin, then part of its back pattern, then the top card's white margin, and then the top card's back pattern. This is different from what they see when the top card is drawn off fairly. So decks such as Aviator and Bicycle are relatively cheatproof as far as bottom-dealing is concerned.

Likewise, any conspicuous, localized design works against bottom-dealing. A prominent design acts as a landmark to help players judge whether the top card is removed. It's best if the design is a different color, such as the logos on some airline and promotional decks. Many Las Vegas casinos use custom Bee decks overprinted with the hotel logos.

Gambling lore favors a United Airlines giveaway deck as the most cheatproof. Flight attendants offer the deck (in first class) or supply it if you know enough to ask for it (in coach). Although manufactured by the U.S. Playing Card Company, the deck is in some ways more secure than that company's popular retail decks. The back design is a solid color except for two United Airlines logos. The white logos make it relatively easy to spot bottom-dealing. The simplicity of the back design makes it nearly impossible to mark the deck. Many other airline decks are equally good.

How to Spot Marked Cards

Any complex back design may be marked. One of only two ink colors—navy blue or medium red—will suffice for the well-known U.S. Playing Card brands. The trouble with marking cards at home, however, is that the deck's seal must be broken.

Premarked cards, favored by serious players, come from Louis Tannen, Inc., a New York magic supply house. Tannen's marked decks are genuine U.S. Playing Card decks that have been opened, marked by hand, and resealed with a duplicate U.S. Playing Card stamp, cellophane wrap, and a white tear-band bearing the brand name. Each deck comes with separate instructions for decoding the markings. *Big Secrets* ordered Tannen's Aviator, Bee, and Bicycle decks to see how the markings are concealed.

Aviator
The markings are along the top margin of the back pattern. Ten "sprout" designs run across the top. The two center sprouts encode the rank. Each sprout has six leaves. One of the leaves is disconnected from the sprout—with a dab of ink—to signify ranks 3 through ace. The leaves on the left side of the left center sprout signify ace, king, and queen, from top to bottom. Leaves on the right side of the left sprout are jack, 10, and 9. Similarly, the right center sprout encodes 8, 7, and 6 and 5, 4, and 3. If no leaf is disconnected, the card is a deuce.

Eight of Hearts

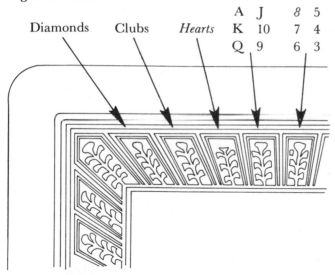

The three sprouts to the left of the center sprouts give the suit. The "bud" at the top of the sprouts is half blocked out to signify (left to right) diamonds, clubs, and hearts. If all the buds are entire, the card is a spade. All the markings are repeated at the bottom, of course, so the cards may be read from either end.

Bee

On all Bee cards, a column of diamond designs runs just inside the right margin. The top three complete diamonds encode the rank. Look at the uppermost of the three diamonds. A triangular extension of dark ink on the right side of the top point of the diamond means ace. A marking on the top left side means king. Similar markings on the bottom point mean queen (bottom left) and jack (bottom right). The diamond below this one encodes 10, 9, 8, and 7; the diamond below that is for 6, 5, 4, and 3. Deuces are not marked.

Ten of Clubs

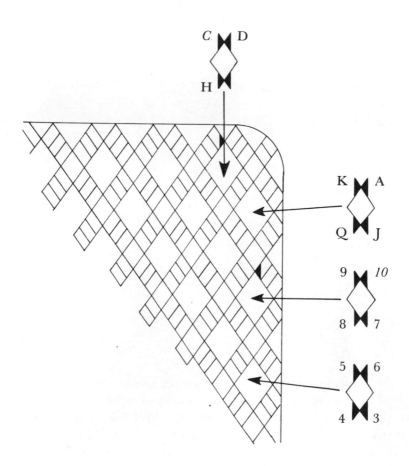

Above and to the left of the upper diamond is another complete diamond. It is for the suits: Top right is diamonds, top left is clubs, and bottom left is hearts. Spades are not marked.

Bicycle

Find the angel in the upper left corner. His left hand rests on a vine that encircles an eight-petal flower design. The flower gives the rank. When the upper (twelve o'clock) petal is narrowed, the card is an ace. Going clockwise, the position of the narrowed petal signifies king (one-thirty), queen (three o'clock), jack (four-thirty), ten (six o'clock), nine (seven-thirty), eight (nine o'clock), and seven (ten-thirty). For lower ranks, the inner tip of the petal is inked out. A truncated petal at twelve o'clock is six; three o'clock is five; six o'clock is four; nine o'clock is three. All the petals are left entire for a deuce.

Ace of Hearts

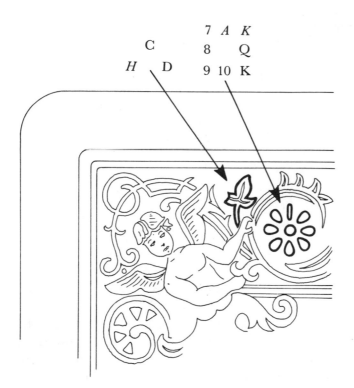

Above the angel's arm is a three-part leaf. When the outer, left tip of the leaf is marked out, the card is a heart. The central, upper tip is for clubs; the inner, right tip is for diamonds; no marking signifies spades.

With sharp eyes the Bicycle and Aviator markings can be read passably well at arm's length. The Bee markings are slightly more difficult to read. Persons aware of the markings but not of their precise location may take several minutes to find the marks.

The Hearts and Diamonds Bomb

Chapter 54 of Tom Robbins' 1980 novel, *Still Life with Woodpecker,* describes a fantastic "hearts and diamonds bomb":

> Take a deck of ordinary playing cards, the old-fashioned paper kind, cut out the red spots and soak them overnight like beans. Alcohol is the best soaking solution, but tap water will suffice. Plug one end of a short length of pipe. Pack the soggy hearts and diamonds into the pipe. On pre-plastic playing cards, the red spots were printed with a diazo dye, a chemical that has an unstable, high-energy bond with nitrogen. So you've got nitro, of sorts, now you'll be needing glycerin. Hand lotion will work nicely. Glug a little lotion into the pipe. To activate the quasi-nitroglycerin, you'll require potassium permanganate. That you can find in the snakebite section of any good first-aid chest. Add a dash of the potassium permanganate and plug the other end of the pipe. Heat the pipe. A direct flame is best, but simply laying the pipe atop a hot radiator will turn the trick. Take cover!

In the context, most readers dismiss this as whimsy. But the hearts and diamonds bomb and the other bombs Robbins describes are real. Similar bomb recipes appear in William Powell's *The Anarchist Cookbook,* an underground weapons manual.

What Robbins calls the "jug band bomb" is a working homemade bomb. It is a glass jug containing a few drops of gasoline. The jug is capped and turned around so the gasoline coats the inner surface and evaporates. A few added drops of potassium permanganate solution make the gasoline vapor/air mixture all the more explosive. The bomb is detonated by throwing or forcibly rolling against a wall.

Whether the hearts and diamonds bomb would work is debatable. Robbins makes certain substitutions in the usual recipe: hand lotion rather than pure glycerin, a snakebite nostrum rather than a potassium permanganate solution of known strength.

Assume then that pure glycerin and potasssium permanganate are used. You might get a bomb by mixing diazo compounds with glycerin and potassium permanganate. The question is how much diazo dye could be extracted from red card spots.

The staff historian for the U.S. Playing Card Company admitted hearing of the bomb stories but was not aware of any working bomb having been constructed. In any case, the main problem with the recipe is that there is nothing "ordinary" about old-fashioned paper playing cards. Effectively all cards are now plastic-coated.

13·

Letters, Stamps, and Envelopes

There is little secret coding or gimmickry on U.S. mail. All U.S. postage stamps have an invisible ink coding that fluoresces in ultraviolet light. Partly this is to deter counterfeiting of stamps. Mostly, it is to speed up sorting. Canceling machines shine an ultraviolet beam on letters and check for a glow. Calcium silicate (which glows orange-red) and zinc orthosilicate (which glows yellow-green) are used. They are printed over the entire surface of stamps or in a geometric pattern.

Personal letters to the U.S. President have a secret numerical code. The President often gets 10,000 letters a day. Virtually all must be opened, read, and answered by the White House mail staff. So that letters from friends get to the President and family unopened, all close friends are given a sequence of numbers to write on the outside of the envelope. The code changes with each President. Ronald Reagan's code was described as a number with a special meaning to Reagan and his wife. Jimmy Carter used an old phone number of Rosalynn's.

Wax Seals

Wax seals are not a guarantee against unauthorized opening of a letter. According to the *CIA Flaps and Seals Manual*, edited by John M. Harrison (Boulder, Colo.: Paladin Press, 1975), there is a way to remove and replace seals.

First the opener takes a plaster-of-Paris cast of the seal. This is set aside to harden. The wax is gently heated with an infrared lamp. When soft, it is rolled into a ball and set aside. The flap of the envelope is steamed open, and the letter is taken out and photocopied.

After the envelope's contents are replaced and the flap resealed, the same wax is used to re-create the seal. It is heated till pliable and pressed back into shape with the plaster-of-Paris mold.

One type of seal is secure, even according to the *CIA Flaps and Seals Manual:* one made of two or more colors of wax melted together. The colors inevitably come out different on the second, surreptitious pressing. But a color Polaroid of the seal must be sent under separate cover so that the recipient can compare it with the seal on the message letter.

None of the other common seals are reliable against unauthorized opening, assuming that knowledgeable letter-openers may want to open your mail. Scotch tape across the flap of an envelope comes off cleanly with carbon tetrachloride (applied with a brush or a hypodermic needle). If you suspect that someone is opening your mail, the manual suggests sending yourself a letter containing a sheet of carbon or wax paper. The heat and mechanical treatment of the letter opening will smudge the carbon and melt the wax. Otherwise, you have to examine letters carefully to detect prior opening. A torn flap, smudging of the flap glue, flattened ridges in the flap, or concave (from the back) curling due to steaming are evidence of opening.

A more sophisticated test requires steaming part of the envelope near the flap for fifteen seconds. Then place the envelope under an ultraviolet lamp. If there is a difference in fluorescence between the steamed and unsteamed part of the envelope, then the envelope paper is suitable for the test. If so, examine the unsteamed part of the flap under the ultraviolet lamp. If it shows a different fluorescence than the other unsteamed parts of the envelope, it indicates that the flap may have been previously steamed.

The ultraviolet lamp is also useful in detecting invisible writing. An effective ultraviolet ink need not fluoresce brightly, as the silicate stamp inks do. Any substance that changes the fluorescence of paper in ultraviolet light yet is invisible in ordinary light will work. Prisoners have used human urine as an invisible ink. Salt water, vinegar, milk, fruit juices, saliva, and water solutions of soap or drugs also work, with varying degrees of legibility.

How to Mail Without a Stamp

Postal chiselers used to mail letters unstamped in the knowledge that they would be delivered anyway—postage due to the recipient. It took a niggardly person to mail personal letters this way, but many people did it on bill payments. So the Post Office changed its policy. It stopped delivering letters without stamps. A letter with a stamp—even a one-cent stamp—is delivered (postage due if need be). A letter with no stamp is returned to the sender.

Naturally, this has just opened up a new way of cheating. Letters can now be mailed for free by switching the positions of the delivery address and the return address. If there is no stamp on the envelope, it will be "returned"—that is, delivered to the address in the upper left corner—which is where the sender wanted it to go in the first place. Unlike under the old system, the letter is not postage-due. At most the recipient gets a stamped purple reminder that "The Post Office does not deliver mail without postage."

At least one large company seems to have adapted this principle to its billing. Citibank bases its MasterCard operations in Sioux Falls, South Dakota. The bill payment envelopes have the Citibank Sioux Falls address in both the delivery address and return address positions. (Most bill payment envelopes have three lines for the customer to write in his return address.) Therefore, regardless of whether the customer puts a stamp on the envelope, it is delivered to Citibank. (The return-address gimmick works even when the return address is in a different state from the mailing point.)

Who is cheating whom? If the customer puts correct postage on the envelope, it is delivered to Sioux Falls at customer expense. No one is slighted. If, on the other hand, the customer intentionally omits the stamp, the payment is delivered at Post Office expense. Then the customer has cheated the Post Office. The Post Office also loses out if the customer honestly forgets to put a stamp on the envelope. But then blame ought to be shared with the peculiar design of Citibank's envelope.

Citibank's motive is plain: If payment envelopes are returned to forgetful customers, it delays payment.

14·

Paraphernalia

A Golf Ball That Cheats

Robinhood is the secret brand of golf ball you may have seen advertised in airline magazines. The brand name "is sealed inside the box, a secret between buyer and seller," says the manufacturer, H&L Labs of Norwalk, Connecticut, in an ad. Why the secrecy? The ball's composition and dimple aerodynamics make it fly farther than regular golf balls. Because it sidesteps USGA specs, it cannot be used legally in play. Yet it looks just like a regular ball. If your partners don't know the secret brand name, no one's the wiser. Coyly hints H&L's pitch, "While golf prides itself on being a gentleman's game, it seems that more than 40,000 gentlemen—and ladies—are playing with these innocent-looking buzz bombs. . . . more money is going to change hands with this little white bandit than all the tournament purses put together."

Secret of a Mail-Order Grooming Aid

Klipette nose-hair clipper, another staple of small mail-order ads in the back of magazines, leads a double life. Apparently, a substantial portion of distributor profits has come from rental of a secret mailing list of Klipette customers.

Figure it this way. Anyone can trim nose hair with ordinary cuticle scissors. Those who feel they must have a special clipper can get one at a drugstore. So the folks responding to Klipette ads include people concerned about nose hair but too embarrassed to face a drugstore clerk and ask for a nose-hair clipper. For whatever reason, that mentality is just right for some direct-mail pitches. According to a Consumers Union report, a Washington financial newsletter reported strong response to a mail subscription campaign directed to Klipette buyers—none of whom suspected where the newsletter got their names.

One of the firms that runs magazine ads for the Klipette is the Complex Company of Waipahu, Hawaii. As an experiment for *Big Secrets,* we ordered the Klipette from the Complex Company, using a fictitious name. That way, any subsequent mail arising from the transaction could be identified. Nothing came for about ten months. Then the fake identity resurfaced with a mailing advertising several products, none of them having much to do with nose hair.

There was a free sample of "Potent-8," a sort of alleged aphrodisiac claimed to "arouse and strip any woman of her normal defenses." The sample smelled like ether.

The mailing touted a book, *Seven Steps to Psychic Mind Control,* that helps the reader "turn women into putty" and "will have YOU scoring at work, parties, or on the streets!"

"Pad-A-Panty" is just what it sounds like, a padded bra for the buttocks ("the easy way to a 'wow' figure that men will notice and women will envy").

The mailing also offered an assortment of weight-loss schemes, including a book, an exercise machine, a body wrap, pills (a "mild stimulant"), and a record or cassette containing subliminal messages to discourage overeating.

The Klipette is not the only mail-order gismo used to create mailing lists. What is remarkable about the Klipette list is the profit picture. The Klipette is manufactured by Hollis Co., a New York cutlery firm, but distributed by various mail-order houses nationwide. The distributor profit on the sale of the Klipette cannot be much. If they clear 6 percent of a typical $2.99 retail price, the profit is only $.18. But each purchase can mean another name on the mailing list. Mailing lists sell for anywhere from $.03 to $.75 a name. With luck, a given list may be sold over and over. Are the Klipette retailers in the business of selling nose-hair clippers, or lists of people who buy nose-hair clippers? Apparently both.

According to Consumers Union, other inexpensive items or services that have been used to build mailing lists include the GI Joe Fan Club (it costs money to join, so the membership roster is a list of kids with big allowances and near-zero sales resistance); Hal-bert's, Inc. (an Ohio firm that sells alleged family coats of arms); the Kozak Drywash (a car-buffing cloth; the Republican Party used a list of buyers to solicit contributions); the "ant certificates" purchasers of ant farms must send in (with their name and address) to get their ants; and many mail-refund or free-product offers.

Toothpaste Horror Stories

Crest toothpaste is the object of two secret-ingredient rumors— one about "sand" and another about "rat poison." Actually, Crest has no secret ingredients other than its flavoring. Everything else is spelled out on the ingredients panel. Among those label ingredients is "hydrated silica." Sand is silica. Crest's silica is certainly processed and finely ground. Ultimately, all industrial silica comes from sand, quartz, or the like. So is there sand in Crest? Well, no, not if you mean grains of silica of the size normally called sand. But yes, if you're willing to trace back the chain of raw materials far enough.

The rat-poison story is likewise a matter of interpretation. Crest used to contain something it called Fluoristan. Fluoristan was a trademarked preparation of stannous fluoride, a chemical that prevents cavities. Then Crest's manufacturers discovered that another fluoride preparation, the one now called Fluoristat, is better at preventing cavities. Out went Fluoristan, and in went Fluoristat. The active ingredient of Fluoristat is sodium fluoride. Sodium fluoride, in turn, is a chemical that otherwise finds use as a rat poison. In fact, sodium fluoride has earned something of a bad name among rat poisons because it is toxic to humans as well as to rats. (It was once mistaken for powdered milk at a hospital for the elderly. The patients complained that breakfast tasted soapy, but no one believed them. Some died.) The level of sodium fluoride in Crest is far below the toxic level, of course.

Wholly untrue are the persistent rumors of a secret significance to the Proctor & Gamble logo on Crest and dozens of other familiar products. A story apparently starting in southern Minnesota in 1980 claims that the moon face symbolizes the acquisition of Proctor & Gamble by Reverend Sun Myung Moon and/or his Unification Church. But the Moonies don't own Procter & Gamble, and the logo has been on Procter & Gamble products for over a century.

A variation of the story finds a secret number in the logo's stars. If you take a pencil and connect the stars properly, the result is three not-very-convincing 6s—the biblical number of the beast and, to believers, evidence of Satanism in Cincinnati. The top five stars become a horizontal 6 (with top at right); the middle four stars form a vertical 6; the bottom four become a rotated 6 dipping slightly below the horizontal. Curved lines and considerable imagination must be used. If you count the stars, the total is thirteen—the head count at the Last Supper.

The Drāno Sex Test

Liquid Drāno, meanwhile, enters into a weird ritual for predicting the gender of an unborn child. The Drackett Company, Drāno's manufacturer, tries to discourage the so-called Drāno sex test. Drāno, after all, is dangerous stuff to be playing around with. During the sixth month of pregnancy, a sample of an expectant mother's morning urine is mixed with an equal amount of Liquid Drāno. The concoction will fizz. The color of the resulting liquid is supposed to predict sex: green for a boy, yellow for a girl. It's right about half the time.

Is the Welcome Hostess a Spy?

Welcome Wagon-*type* services are sometimes spies for credit bureaus. Newcomers are a problem for credit reporters. They're the people creditors are most likely to want information on and yet the people most likely to have an empty file. Most welcome services have names patterned after "Welcome Wagon," but not all are affiliated with Welcome Wagon International. Many services are sponsored by the local credit bureau, which hopes you'll tell the smiling Welcome Hostess why you really had to leave town.

Telltale White Lines

Chevrolet, Buick, and Cadillac odometers cannot be rolled back—at least not without it being apparent to any used-car dealer. Since 1969 General Motors cars have had two thin white plastic flags, normally held out of view by a seal, in the odometer case. Tampering with the odometer breaks the seal, and the flags drop into view. They appear as two telltale vertical lines on either side of the thousands' digit—for example, 3|1|820.1.

GM dealers seem to have benefited most from the device. Few customers know what to look for. Absence of the lines is no guarantee of accurate milage. Dealers can buy replacement seals (from independent manufacturers, not GM) to conceal the lines on a doctored car.

Bizarre Hair Treatment

Tia Zolin Placenta, a hair conditioner used in many salons, is said to come from human placentas. It is a straw-colored liquid—with a white sediment—that comes in a single-use sealed vial. The vial is shaken and broken in a towel. The liquid is massaged into the hair. It is not rinsed out—if there really is placenta in Tia Zolin, it is in the hair of anyone who has just used it.

Where do they get human placentas? Tia Zolin Placenta is manufactured by Hask, Inc., of Great Neck, New York. In response to a letter asking about the product, a Hask vice-president confirmed that there is human material in Tia Zolin. But what they call placenta comes from human umbilical cords, not placentas per se. Hask says it gets the umbilical cords from hospitals "in much the same way that human blood and other vital organs are obtained."

Secret Store

Gucci shops have a secret store-within-a-store, the Galeria. Located in the major U.S. Gucci outlets, the Galeria is on a floor of its own above street level. In New York, for instance, it's the fourth floor of the 2 East 54th Street shop. To keep out hoi polloi, the Galeria is accessible only by elevator, and you need a special gold key to get to the right floor. Gucci distributes the gold keys to its best customers. (If you push the floor number of the Galeria without inserting the key, the elevator doesn't move.) Galeria merchandise runs heavily toward jewelry in the high five-figure range.

Secret Bank

Bank of America's Beverly Hills, California, branch at 9461 Wilshire Boulevard has much the same thing—a hush-hush department upstairs for its wealthiest depositors, with no waiting in line for tellers.

Secret Restaurant

Ma Maison, Los Angeles' celebrity eatery at 8368 Melrose Boulevard, keeps out the triptik-and-Bryce-Canyon-decal crowd with an unlisted phone number: (213) 655-1991.

Secret Airline Club

Northwest Orient Airlines' "club" has visibility zero. Like most of the airline clubs, Northwest's "Top Flight Lounges" were started as a free perk for heavy travelers and those in a position to help the airline—corporate travel directors, Civil Aeronautics Board officials, celebrities who might be photographed coming off a plane. In 1966 the CAB decided such invitation-only clubs were unfair. Most airlines started publicizing their clubs, opening them to anyone, and tacking on an annual or lifetime membership fee. But Northwest (and until 1982, Delta) chose not to publicize its club. Officially Northwest's club is not a club at all but a set of free lounges for the enjoyment of all persons holding Northwest tickets. The catch is, Northwest has never made it easy for average passengers to learn where the Top Flight Lounges are— or even that there are such lounges. The lounges are said to be hidden away behind nondescript doors or in airport culs-de-sac. Unless someone with the airline decides that you're Northwest's kind of person, you're on your own.

Suspect Luggage

Samsonite luggage may be prone to extra scrutiny from customs inspectors. The reason is a South American brand of luggage, Saxony, that looks just like Samsonite but features a false bottom that can be used for drugs or other contraband.

Indiscreet Typewriter Ribbon

IBM typewriter ribbon is a boon to industrial spies: The used plastic ribbon contains a razor-sharp impression of everything typed. And only the top-level correspondence is likely to be typed on one-use ribbon. That makes sifting through corporate trash bins all the easier.

Bugs in Books

Tattle-Tape is the name of the bookstore security system requiring electronic detectors at the exits and a rectangular "desensitizer" at the cashier stands. The customer is given to understand that each book must be passed, spine down, over the desensitizer to prevent tripping the alarm. Yet if you've ever searched for an electronic bug in the spine after buying a book, you probably didn't find anything.

The secret of the Tattle-Tape system is that there isn't anything to find in most of the protected inventory. It is a spot-check system. Only a few selected books contain the Tattle-Tape strip. The strip is thin, brownish, and self-adhesive. It is not placed inside the book's spine but rather on one of the pages, as close to the spine as possible. The routine of passing every book over the desensitizer is mainly a deterrent. Desensitized or not, the books not containing a strip can be carted out by the wheelbarrow without setting off the alarm.

The 3M Company, Tattle-Tape's manufacturer, is close-mouthed about the mechanics of the system. The Tattle-Tape seems plainly to be a magnetic strip. If so, it could probably be erased with a pocket magnet. That, perhaps, is what the desensitizer does. Those who purchase a book with a strip may find it objectionable and hard to remove. For this reason, and the labor costs of placing the strips, bookstore managers try to avoid using the strips except where most necessary. Promotional literature of the 3M Company advises using Tattle-Tape strips in "high-theft books," "books near doors," and "volumes over $20.00."

A bookstore using the Tattle-Tape system may return unsold books—with active strips—to their publishers. The publishers, in turn, may ship these books to different stores that don't have the Tattle-Tape system. Books sold at these stores will not be desensitized. If the purchasers take their books into another store or a library, they may trip the alarm system—and be at a loss to explain what has happened.

PART FOUR

Alice, Let's Cheat

L ife is short. One minute you're doing your stretching exercises. The next thing you know, your next of kin are dividing your good silverware. Once it's finally time to roll over and play Parvovirus, you may not care how many Brownie points you racked up for citizenship. In fact, you'll probably wish you stepped on more people as you clawed your way to the top. Here then is a start. There are plenty of annoying tests you have to take after college, and you might as well start cheating on them. Thanks to convenient glitches in test security, some of these post-curricular pop quizzes can be reproduced here with answers—a sort of Cliff's Notes for life. No talking; pencils down; this may go on your permanent record. Please begin.

15·

The Eye Test

Does the optometrist swap answered-the-waffle-iron jokes with the receptionist as soon as you're out of earshot? You never really know because it's not considered good optometric bedside manner to tell the examinee how far down the chart he or she is supposed to be able to read. To qualify for 20/20 vision, you have to be able to read line 8 at the customary examination distance of twenty feet. It's the line just above the red bar: DEFPOTEC. Some slack is built into the definition of normal vision, so many people can read line 9 as well, especially if the light is good.

Helpful hint: only nine letters are used in the standard Snellen eye chart. All occur at least once in easy lines 1 through 5. So if you think you see a G down in the fine print, it's a C or an O.

Want to show off? The bottom line is PEZOLCFTD.

	E	1
	F P	2
	T O Z	3
	L P E D	4
	P E C F D	5
	E D F C Z P	6
	F E L O P Z D	7
	D E F P O T E C	8
	L E F O D P C T	9
	F D P L T C E O	10
	P E Z O L C F T D	11

16·

The Rorschach Test

Most people have heard of the Rorschach test, but few have ever seen a real Rorschach inkblot. The blots are kept secret. When you see an inkblot in a popular article on the test (as in the *Encyclopaedia Britannica* entry on the Rorschach test), it's a fake: *an* inkblot, but not one of *the* inkblots. There are only ten Rorschach inkblots.

Psychologists want the blots to remain a secret from the general public so that reactions to the blots will be spontaneous. Hermann Rorschach hoped these spontaneous reactions would yield valuable clues to the test subject's personality. Whether they do remains controversial. Many psychologists think the Rorschach test is hopelessly unreliable; others see it as one of the cardinal tools of modern psychodiagnosis. Even among those who acknowledge the value of the test, there is disagreement on interpretation of responses.

Just as secret as the blots themselves are the ground rules for administering the test. There are a few things that you, as a subject, are supposed to know and a lot of things you aren't supposed to know. If you ask about something you're not supposed to know, the psychologist will give you a pat answer as prescribed in Rorschach literature. For example, if you ask if it is okay to turn the card upside down, the psychologist will respond that you may do as you like; it's up to you. The psychologist won't say that many of the cards are easier to interpret when turned; that most people do turn the cards; that he or she will make a notation with a little arrowhead every time you do turn a card; and that you lose points in the initiative department if you don't turn the cards.

You'll be handed the cards one by one in the fixed order devised by Rorschach (there are numbers on the backs of the cards for the psychologist's benefit). The first card, for instance, looks like a fox's head or a jack-o'-lantern. The cards are thick, rectangular cardboard, 6⅝ inches by 9½ inches. Half of the blots are black ink on a white background. Two others are black and red ink on white, and the last three blots are multicolored. The psychologist will always put each card in your hands "right" side up.

You aren't supposed to know it, but the psychologist will write down everything you say. This includes any seemingly irrelevant questions you may have. To keep you from getting wise, the psychologist always arranges to sit to your side and a little behind you, so that you can't look at the card and the psychologist at the same time. Most subjects realize the psychologist is taking notes, of course, but they don't realize that the notes are a special shorthand record of *everything* said. Some psychologists use hidden tape recorders.

The psychologist will also time how long it takes you to respond, using a "tickless" watch. The psychologist will not ask you to hurry up or slow down and will not make any reference to time, but response times (in seconds) are one of the things he or she is writing in the notes.

Don't hold the card at an unusual angle. Watch how you phrase things. Say "This looks like . . ." or "This could be . . ." never "This is . . ." After all, you're supposed to realize that it is just a blot of ink on a card. By the same token, don't be too literal and say things as, "This is a blotch of black ink." Don't groan, get emotional, or make irrelevant comments. Don't put your hands on the cards to block out parts. The psychologist will watch for all of the foregoing as signs of brain damage.

If there are no right answers for the test, there are some general guidelines as to what is a normal response. You can probably see images in the inkblots proper and in the white spaces they enclose. Stick to the former. Don't be afraid of being obvious. There are several responses that almost everyone gives; mentioning these shows the psychologist you're a regular guy.

It is okay to be original if you can justify what you see in the shape, shading, or color of the blot. If you see an abalone and can point out why it looks like one, then say so. Justifiable original responses are usually judged to be indicative of creativity or intelligence. You don't want *non sequiturs,* images that don't fit the blot in the judgment of the psychologist. These may be signs of psychosis.

You're expected to see more than one thing on all or most of the cards. Not being able to see anything on a card suggests neurosis. Usually the more things you can see, the better, as long as they fit the form and color of the blot. Of course, you can see things in the whole blot or in parts of it, and images may overlap.

Since time is a factor, it is important to come up with good answers fast. (It looks particularly bad if you take a long time and give a dumb, inappropriate answer.) The most reliable way to come up with good answers is to memorize what the good answers are. Copyright restrictions prevent us from showing you the blots themselves, so we'll use outlines. We'll refer to the blots as psychologists do, as Plates I through X. The psychologist won't mention the numbers to you, but the blots will always be in order.

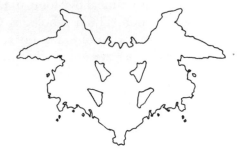

Plate I

Black ink. A roughly triangular shape, point down, suggesting a broad, fox-like face with prominent ears. Naughty bits: a pair of breasts (rounded projections at top of blot); a vertical female figure, her torso partly visible through a gauzy dress (along center line).

The first blot is easy. How fast you answer is taken as an indication of how well you cope with new situations. The best reaction is to give one of the most common responses immediately. Good answers are bat, butterfly, moth, and (in center of blot) a female figure. Mask, jack-o'-lantern, and animal face are common responses too, but in some interpretation schemes they suggest paranoia. A bad response is any that says something untoward about the central female figure. "She" is often judged to be a projection of your own self-image. Avoid the obvious comment that the figure has two breasts but no head.

If you don't give more than one answer for Plate I, many psychologists will drop a hint—tell you to look closer.

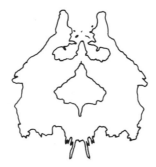

Plate II

Black and red ink. Two dark-gray splotches suggesting dancing figures. Red splotches at top of each figure and at bottom center. Naughty bits: penis (upper center, black ink); vagina (the red area at bottom center).

It is important to see this blot as two human figures—usually females or clowns. If you don't, it's seen as a sign that you have trouble relating to people. You may give other responses as well, such as cave entrance (the triangular white space between the two figures) and butterfly (the red "vagina," bottom center).

Should you mention the penis and vagina? Not necessarily. Every Rorschach plate has at least one obvious representation of sexual anatomy. You're not expected to mention them all. In some interpretation schemes, mentioning more than four sex images in the ten plates is diagnostic of schizophrenia. The trouble is, subjects who took Psychology 101 often assume they should detail every possible sex response, so allowances must be made. Most Rorschach workers believe the sex images should play a part in the interpretation of responses even when not mentioned. You may not say that the lower red area looks like a vagina, but psychologists assume that what you do say will show how you feel about women. Nix on "crab"; stick with "butterfly."

Plate III

Black and red ink. Two obvious figures (black ink) facing each other. But-terfly-shaped red blot between the figures; an elongated red blot behind each figure's head. Naughty bits: penises and breasts (at anatomically appropri-ate positions for each figure).

This is the blot that supposedly can determine sexual prefer-ence. Most people see the two human figures. Both figures have prominent "breasts" and an equally prominent "penis." If you don't volunteer the gender of the figures, you'll be asked to specify it. By the traditional interpretation, seeing the figures as male is a heterosexual response (for test subjects of both sexes). Describing the figures as female or acknowledging the androgynous nature of the blot is supposed to be a homosexual response. Does it work? Not really—many straights describe the figures as women, and not all gays give a gay response. A 1971 study at Mount Sinai Hospital in New York showed the traditionally heterosexual re-sponse (two male figures) to be declining in popularity.

The splotches of red ink are usually perceived separately. Com-mon responses are bow tie or ribbon (inner red area) and a stom-ach and esophagus (outer red areas).

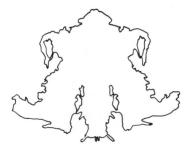

Plate IV

Black ink. A roughly triangular blot, point up, with the two lower corner regions resembling boots or feet. Naughty bits: two penises (on either side of blot, near top of triangle); vagina (on center line near top of blot).

Plate IV is the "father card." At first glance it is a difficult blot to see as a single image. The "boots" are fairly conspicuous; between them is the apparent head of a dog or Chinese dragon. Many subjects see the blot as an animal skin. After a few seconds, though, most can see it as a standing figure seen from below. The boots become the feet, enlarged because of the unusual perspective. The arms and head, at the top, are smaller. Common descriptions are bear, gorilla, or man in a heavy coat. Bad descriptions are monster or *attacking* bear or gorilla—Rorschach theorists equate your description of the figure with your perception of your father or male authority figures.

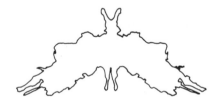

Plate V

Black ink. A simple, batlike shape. Naughty bits: two penises (the "ears" or "antennae").

Rorschach himself thought this was the easiest blot to interpret. It is a bat or a butterfly, period. You don't want to mention anything else. Seeing the projections on the ends of the bat wings as crocodile heads signifies hostility. Seeing the paired butterfly antennae or feet as scissors or pliers signifies a castration complex. Schizophrenics sometimes see moving people in this blot.

Many psychologists take particular note of the number of responses given to this plate. If you mention more images here than in either Plate IV or VI, it is suggestive of schizophrenia.

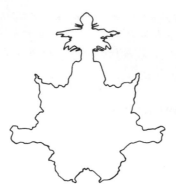

Plate VI

Black ink. An irregular shape like that of an animal-skin rug. Naughty bits: penis (center line at top); vagina (below penis).

Plate VI is the most difficult blot. The best-rendered penis of all the blots is at top, but few subjects mention it. The rest of the blot doesn't look like much of anything. Some hold that the value of this blot is to have the subject grope for images and possibly reveal subconscious attitudes about sexuality.

Basically, the secret of this plate is to turn it. A good response is to say it looks like an animal hide (about the only reasonable response when held right side up), then turn it on its side and say it looks like a boat or surfaced submarine with reflection, and then turn it upside down and say it looks like a mushroom cloud, a pair of theater masks, or caricatures of men with long noses and goatees.

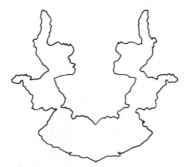

Plate VII

Black ink. A U-shaped blot, each side of the U resembling a female figure in a narrow-waisted dress. Naughty bits: a vagina (on center line at bottom of U).

Christina Crawford meets projective psychology: This blot is supposed to reveal how you really feel about your mother. Virtually everyone sees two girls or women. Deprecating descriptions of the figures—"witches," "gossips," "girls fighting," "spinsters"—indicate poor maternal relations. Seeing the blot as thunderclouds instead of female figures suggests anxiety to some psychologists; seeing it as a walnut kernel may mean a vulvar fixation.

There is an entirely different side to this blot, but you're not supposed to see it. The white space between the girls or women can be interpreted as an oil lamp or similar object. It is claimed that only schizophrenics usually see the lamp.

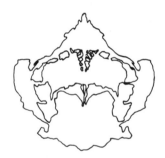

Plate VIII

Pink, blue, gray, and orange ink. An almost circular array of interconnected forms—a gray triangle (point up) at top, a pair of blue rectangles in the center, a pink and orange splotch at bottom, and two pink "animal" shapes forming the right and left sides of the circle. Naughty bits: a vagina (pink-orange area at bottom).

The first full-color card is easy. It is important that you see the four-legged animals—lions, pigs, bears, etc.—on the sides of the blot. They're one of the most common responses on the test, and you're assumed to be a mental defective if you don't see them. Other good responses are tree (gray triangle at top), butterfly (pink and orange area at bottom), and rib cage or anatomy chart (skeletal pattern in center between blue rectangles and gray triangles). The entire configuration can be seen as a heraldic design (good answer) or a Christmas tree with ornaments (reaching). Children tend to like this blot and say a lot about it—the bright colors and animal shapes make it more interesting than your basic penis/vagina number (II, IV, or VI).

Plate IX

Green, orange, and pink ink. A very irregular upright rectangle. Orange at top, protruding green areas at center, pink at bottom. Naughty bits: a vagina (center line at bottom).

There aren't many good answers here. If you're going to throw up your hands (figuratively; see warning about emotional outbursts above) and plead a mental block, this is the place to do it.

The colors clash, apparently by Rorschach's design. Good answers are a fire with smoke, an explosion (but paranoids are claimed more apt to note the pale green mushroom cloud on the center line at top), a map, anatomy, or a flower. If you turn the card ninety degrees, you can make out a man's head in the pink areas at bottom. (The man is identified as Mark Twain, Santa Claus, or Teddy Roosevelt.) A bad response is to describe the orange areas at top as monsters or men fighting—a sign of poor social development. As with Plate V, the psychologist may be counting the number of responses you give to this blot for comparison with the preceding and succeeding blots. You want to give fewer responses to this blot.

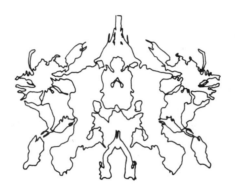

Plate X

Pink, blue, gray, green, yellow, and orange ink. A loose assortment of brightly colored shapes, the most chaotic of the plates. Naughty bits: penis and testes (top center, gray ink).

The unspoken purpose of this last blot is to test your organizational ability. Plate X is full of colorful odds and ends easy to identify—blue spiders, gray crabs, paired orange maple seeds, green caterpillars, a light-green rabbit's head, yellow and orange fried eggs—and you're expected to list them. But the psychologist will also be looking for a comprehensive answer, something that shows you grok the whole *Gestalt.* There are two good holistic answers: sea life and a view through a microscope.

Some subjects see two reddish faces at top center, separated by the orange maple key. If you describe them as blowing bubbles or smoking pipes, it may be interpreted as evidence of an oral fixation. Seeing the gray "testes" and "penis" as two animals eating a stick or tree indicates castration anxiety.

17·

The Lie-Detector Test

The polygraph was invented by William Moulton Marston, who was, strangely enough, also the creator of the *Wonder Woman* comic strip (under the name Charles Moulton). The standard polygraph records only three distinct vital signs. A blood-pressure cuff on the upper arm measures changes in blood pressure. Wires attached to the fingers measure changes in electrical resistance of the skin due to sweating. Rubber straps around the torso measure the breathing rate. This information is displayed as four squiggles on a moving strip of graph paper.

Whether or not you believe a polygraph provides useful information (most psychologists have their doubts), there is a good chance you'll be asked to take a polygraph test. The vast majority of lie-detector tests are administered for employee screening—"Have you been using the WATS line for personal calls?" and so forth—not for police work. In *A Tremor in the Blood: Uses and Abuses of the Lie Detector* (New York: McGraw-Hill, 1981), polygraph critic David Thoreson Lykken estimates that as many as one million polygraph examinations are performed on Americans each year. In criminal cases, even the manifestly innocent may be asked to take a polygraph test. All Yakima County, Washington, rape victims are required to take the test; refusal means the case will not be prosecuted.

At best, all the polygraph can indicate is a heightened emotional reaction to a question. It cannot specify what kind of an emotional reaction. Polygraphers try to design question formats so guilt-induced nervousness will be the only emotion invoked and so the subject's reaction to relevant questions can be compared to other, "control" questions.

The Lie-Control Test

This is the question format used in most police investigations. It usually starts with a card trick devised by two pioneer polygraphers, John E. Reid and F. E. Inbau.

The polygrapher hooks the subject to the polygraph and takes out a deck of cards. The polygrapher tells the subject that he must "calibrate" the polygraph with a simple test. He fans the deck and asks the subject to select a card. The subject is told to look at the card but not to show it or mention its name. The polygrapher tells the subject to answer "no" to every question asked about the card. "Is it a black card?" the polygrapher asks. "Is it a high card?" and so on. After each "no" the polygrapher scrutinizes the tracings and fiddles with the dials. If the no answer is incorrect, the polygrapher disagrees. The field is soon narrowed to one card—and it is the correct card.

Needless to say, the polygrapher uses a trick deck. The point is to foster confidence in the machine. After identifying the card, the polygrapher comments that the subject's reactions are particularly easy to read and segues into the interrogation.

Three types of questions are used in a lie-control test. The entire list is read to the subject well in advance of the test. The start of a typical interrogation might run like this:

1. Is your name Sarah Elkins?
2. Is Paris the capital of France?
3. Have you ever failed to report more than fifty dollars of tip, gambling, or gift income on a single year's tax return?
4. Is this apple red?
5. Do you have any idea why the cash receipts for the last quarter are about twenty-two thousand dollars in error?
6. Is there something important that you did not mention on your job application?
7. Have you been embezzling from the company?

The first question is always irrelevant to the matter being investigated. It has to be because many subjects get nervous on the first question no matter what. Other irrelevant questions are asked throughout the interrogation (questions 2 and 4 in the sample list). If the subject gives any thought to these questions, he assumes that they are control questions to provide a yardstick for evaluating responses to the relevant questions. Actually, the irrelevant questions are there to give the subject's vital signs time to return to normal. They aren't the control questions.

Questions 5 and 7 in the list above are relevant questions—the only questions the examiner is really interested in. The relevant questions are asked in several different wordings during the test.

Questions 3 and 6 are control questions. In the pretest discussion of the questions, the polygrapher explains that it is helpful to throw in a few "general honesty" questions. Whoever committed the serious crime, the spiel goes, probably committed less serious crimes in the past. Hence the inclusion of questions about tax cheating, lying on job applications, stealing as a child, etc.

The polygrapher affects the attitude that it would be damaging indeed to admit to any such indiscretions. Frequently this scares the subject into admitting minor crimes. In that case, the polygrapher frowns and agrees to rewrite the question. Should the subject concede failing to report eighty dollars in gambling winnings, question 3 might be changed to "Have you ever failed to report more than a hundred dollars of tip, gambling, or gift income on a single year's tax return?" If necessary, several of the control questions may be reworded before the test—always so that the subject will be able to give the "honest" response.

In reality, the whole point of each control question is to manufacture a lie. It is the secret working premise of polygraphers that everyone commits the minor transgressions that are the subject of the usual control questions. All the subject's denials on the control questions are assumed to be lies. The polygraph tracings during these "lies" establish a base line for interpreting the reaction to the relevant questions.

The reason for rewriting some control questions is so a candid subject will not admit to minor crimes on the test. That would be telling the truth, and the polygrapher wants the subject to lie. The control questions are intentionally broad. Even if a question is reworded to exclude the confessed instance, it is assumed that any denial must be a lie.

The rationale for the lie-control test goes like this: The honest subject will be worried about the control questions. He'll know that he has committed small transgressions or suspect that he must have, even if he can't remember them. So he'll be afraid that the machine will detect his deception on the "general honesty" questions (especially in view of its success with the card trick). That would be embarrassing at least, and it might throw suspicion on him for the larger crime. In contrast, the relevant questions should be less threatening to the honest subject. He knows he didn't commit the crimes they refer to.

The guilty person, on the other hand, should have far more to fear from the relevant questions. If the machine can detect lying on the relevant issue, it matters little that it might also implicate him in petty matters.

By this hypothesis, an innocent person should have greater polygraphic response to the control questions than to the relevant questions. The guilty pattern is just the reverse: greater response to the relevant questions. This, at any rate, is what polygraphers look for when the machine is switched on.

The Relevant-Control Test

The relevant-control test is the type used for most employee screenings. Thus it is the most common type of examination. The interrogation consists only of irrelevant and relevant questions. As with the lie-control test, the first question and a few others are irrelevant. The relevant questions usually test workplace honesty: "Have you ever taken home office supplies for personal use?" "Have you ever clocked in for someone else?"

The premise is that no one will lie about everything. So if a few of the relevant questions produce heightened responses, they are presumed to be the questions on which the subject is lying. Unfortunately, there is no unambiguous way of deciding how much response indicates a lie. Most psychologists agree that the relevant-control test is a poor test of deception.

The Reid/Inbau card trick is eliminated from employee screenings: There is too great of chance of coworkers comparing notes and discovering that everyone picked the ace of spades.

How to Beat the Lie Detector

To the extent that the polygraph works at all, it works because people believe it does. Many criminals confess during polygraph examinations. Many employees are more honest for fear of periodic screenings. But a dummy polygraph that hummed and scribbled preprogrammed tracings would be no less effective in these instances.

David Thoreson Lykken estimates that lie-control polygraph tests are about 70 percent accurate. (Remember, though, that choosing "heads" or "tails" of a flipped coin can be accurate 50 percent of the time.) Accuracy of 70 percent is not impressive, but it is high enough to talk meaningfully of beating a polygraph test.

Just by having read this far, you stand a greater chance of beating a polygraph test. You won't be wowed by the card demonstration. You realize that the polygraph's powers are limited. There are two additional techniques for beating the polygraph. The more obvious is to learn how to repress physiologic responses to stressful questions. Some people are good at this; others are not. Most people can get better by practicing with a polygraph. Of course, this training requires a polygraph, and polygraphs are expensive.

The opposite approach is to pick out the control questions in the pretest discussion and exaggerate reactions to these questions during the test. When the control-question responses are greater than the relevant-question responses, the polygrapher must acquit the subject.

Because breathing is one of the parameters measured, taking a deep breath and holding it will record as an abnormal response. Flexing the arm muscles under the cuff distorts the blood-pressure reading. But a suspicious polygrapher may spot either ruse.

A more subtle method is to hide a tack in one shoe. Stepping on the tack during the control questions produces stress reactions with no outward signs of fidgeting. Biting the tongue forcefully also works.

18·

How to Crash
the Freemasons

Masonry swears its members to secrecy with grisly, anatomically explicit oaths. A Master Freemason must "promise and swear, that I will not write, print, stamp, stain, hew, cut, carve, indent, paint, or engrave" the mysteries of his order "under no less penalty than to have my throat cut across, my tongue torn out by the roots, and my body buried in the rough sands of the sea," according to one version of the oath. Tenth-degree Masons "consent to have my body opened perpendicularly, and to be exposed for eight hours in the open air, that the venomous flies may eat my entrails" if they talk. Even the Shriners, a "fun" order, may incur "the fearful penalty of having my eyeballs pierced to the center with a three-edged blade."

Be that as it may, the secrets of the Masons are preserved in certain arcane tracts, pamphlets, and books. These are sold only by Masonic supply houses—the firms that sell fezzes, banners, plaques, jewels, and other regalia to lodges. The supply houses take the secrecy seriously. Most will not sell booklets containing club secrets to anyone who cannot show a Masonic ID. *Big Secrets* came across a Chicago firm, however, that works by mail order. The Geo. Lauterer Corporation publishes an illustrated catalog of lodge gear. It offers over a hundred Masonic and other fraternal manuscripts. We obtained a sampling of titles.

American Masonry differs in certain particulars from British or Continental Masonry. Rituals may vary from lodge to lodge. Masonic tracts do not always agree. Except where noted, the information below is taken from two of Lauterer's titles, *Richardson's Monitor of Freemasonry* by a pseudonymous Benjamin Henry Day, and *Initiation Stunts* by Lieutenant Beale Cormack.

The Secret Handshake

It's a regular handshake, except that you press your forefinger hard into the other's palm. The thumb presses against the base joints of the second and third fingers. It looks pretty much like any other handshake; only the persons shaking hands can feel the difference.

The Secret Password

"Tubal-Cain" (too̅·bəl·kān′) is the secret password of a Master Mason. But some lodges have their own passwords.

The Secret Word

Not to be confused with the password. The Word (always capitalized) is so secret that initiates are taught it one letter at a time. First they learn A, then O, then M, and finally I. The Word is IAOM.

You never get a straight story as to what it means. As best as anyone can figure, it is the ineffable name of God, or some approximation thereof. The Word (or Name) is a tongue-twister. It takes some practice to get it right. The following pronunciation guide is from *Masonry and Its Symbols in the Light of Thinking and Destiny* by Harold Waldwin Percival:

> The Name is pronounced as follows: It is started by opening the lips with an "ee" sound graduating into a broad "a" as the mouth opens wider with lips forming an oval shape and then graduating the sound to "o" as the lips form a circle, and again modulating to an "m" sound as the lips close to a point. This point resolves itself to a point within the head.
>
> Expressed phonetically the Name is "EE-Ah-Oh-Mmm" and is pronounced with one continuous out-breathing with a slight nasal tone in the manner described above. It can be correctly and properly expressed with its full power only by one who has brought his physical body to a state of perfection . . .

The Secret Code

The Freemasons' cipher is rarely used, but it is mentioned in several sources. You make a diagram like this:

A	B	C
D	E	F
G	H	I

N	O	P
Q	R	S
T	U	V

Each letter is encoded by drawing its cell in the diagram. MASON becomes

The Shriners' Recognition Test

According to a Lauterer manuscript, this is how two Shriners recognize each other:

Q. Then I presume you are a Noble?
A. I am so accepted by all men of noble birth.
Q. Have you traveled any?
A. I have.
Q. From where to what place have you traveled?
A. Traveled east over the hot burning sands of the desert.
Q. Where were you stopped at?
A. At the devil's pass.
Q. What were you requested to do?
A. I was requested to contribute a few drops of urine.
Q. Why were you requested to do this?
A. As a token of my renouncing the wiles and evils of the world and granted permission to worship at the Shrine.
Q. At what Shrine did you worship?
A. At the Shrine of Islam.
Q. Did you ride?
A. Yes, I rode a camel until I paused to dismount.
Q. Then what did you do with your camel?
A. I tied him.
Q. Where did you tie him?

A. I tied him to a date tree, where all True Shriners should
do so.

BOTH: Yes, I pulled the Cord, rode the hump, I have tra-
versed the hot arid sands of the desert to find Peace and
rest in the quiet shades of the Oasis.

Initiation

There are two sides to Freemason initiations—one a standardized,
sedate ritual; the other a highly variable set of hazing stunts.

Prospective Masons must apply of their own free will. Masons
may not recruit their friends, at least not in theory. Proposed
members are investigated by a committee of lodge members. This
is often just a formality but may include, for instance, a credit report. The committee reports on the candidate at a lodge meeting.
Members then vote.

The ballot box in the Lauterer catalog uses white balls and
black cubes. (Losers are blackcubed, not blackballed.) If there is a
single negative vote, the ballot is declared foul. The lodgemaster
(who sees how each member voted) may try to convince dissent-
ing members to reconsider. A negative verdict on the second ballot is final.

Successful candidates are invited to the lodge for initiation.
There are three basic degrees: Entered Apprentice, Fellow Craft,
and Master Mason. Each has its own ritual.

Entered Apprentice candidates begin by taking off their clothes
to prove their gender (women may not become Masons). In practice, this means taking off the pants and any jacket. Underwear
and shirt are kept on, but the shirt is unbuttoned and pulled
down to bare the left arm, shoulder, and breast.

The candidate is hoodwinked (blindfolded). A cabletow (rope)
is placed around the neck. (The Lauterer catalog's hoodwink is
simply a standard, black satin half-face mask—without eye-
holes—secured with an elastic string. The cabletow is a heavy
blue rayon cord with tassels at both ends.) Ideally, the cabletow is
supposed to have four strands to symbolize the four senses (they
don't count touch). The candidate is escorted to a room where
three candles are burning. One of the lodge members takes a
mason's compass or other sharp instrument and pricks the candidate's bared skin. The candidate is instructed to recite a formula

to the effect that what he desires most is light. The other lodge members remove his hookwink and cabletow. Before the candidate are the three candles. He is told that the candles represent the sun, the moon, and the master of the lodge.

The candidate gets a lecture on the symbolism of Masonry. Visual aids are used (Lauterer sells a set of three lecture charts and a set of 118 35-millimeter slides). He is given a "lambskin," a white apron. Lauterer's lambskins are indeed genuine lambskin, lined with cotton. They measure 13 inches by 15 inches or 14 inches by 16 inches. A triangular flap folds down like the flap of an envelope. The lambskin is worn in front, and a tie (tape or cord with tassels) fastens behind the back.

A member of the lodge pretends to be a collector for a needy cause and asks the candidate to donate. Lacking his wallet, the candidate must refuse. The moral: Help the less fortunate. Then the candidate is allowed to put his clothes back on. He is taken before the master of the lodge. The master tells him that he is now a Mason. The candidate is given the working tools of the Apprentice, a twenty-four-inch gauge and a gavel.

The second and third degrees follow a similar pattern. Both repeat the business with the hoodwink and the cabletow. For the Fellow Craft initiation, the right shoulder is bared, and the cabletow is tied around the right biceps. In the Master Mason initiation, the cabletow is wound around the body three times. Each degree has its own lecture on symbolism.

Then there are optional degrees. Their initiation rituals take the form of short plays starring the candidate and other lodge members. The playlets deal with incidents from the mythic history of the Masons, such as the building of King Solomon's Temple and the murder of Temple architect Hiram Abiff. These initiations cost the candidate about $150 a pop, so any thirty-second-degree Mason has dropped over $4,000. Once a Mason has completed the twenty-nine optional degrees of the Scottish rite or the six optional degrees of the York rite, he is eligible to become a Shriner—which means still another initiation.

Depending on the whim of other lodge members, initiations may include a set of burlesque tests to prove a candidate's mettle. These blend sophomoric practical jokes, soft S&M, and an electric carpet (the latter "just the item for initiations," touts the Lauterer catalog, at $4.75 a square foot; jump spark battery extra). Lauterer's *Initiation Stunts* booklet describes over thirty tests judged suitable for fraternal orders, of which the following is a sample. In all cases, candidates are blindfolded. Here's how the Masons keep out the wimps:

"Chewing the Rag"
A lodge member criticizes two candidates for speaking: "They both talk too much and I fear they will someday betray the secrets of our brotherhood." As a lesson, the candidates must "chew the rag." The member says that he has a six-foot length of string with a raisin tied in the middle. Each candidate gets an end of the string. The member instructs the candidates to chew the string from their respective ends: The one who gets the raisin will be excused from "The Test of the Drowning Man." They chew. The "raisin" is really a piece of candy coated with Epsom salts. There is no "Test of the Drowning Man."

"Oriental Dance"
Lodge members strip a candidate and put a skirt on him. As Oriental music is played, he is forced to dance on the electric carpet. This is one of several uses of the carpet, all of which are deemed more effective if the candidate does not know about the carpet. The electric-shock sensation is not immediately identifiable as such, or so the semiwarped reasoning goes. Members may warn the blindfolded candidate to "step high" to avoid burning desert sands, barbed wire, or snakebites.

"A Trip to the Moon"
A member raps his gavel and orders all to be seated. A second member replies that there is no seat for himself and one of the candidates. They are told to sit on the floor. They sit on a spread blanket. As soon as the candidate is seated, the second member steps off the blanket. The candidate is told to sing a song. The lodge members protest his singing and demand that he be punished. All quietly grab the ends of the blanket and toss the candidate in the air.

"The Barber Shop"
A member feels a candidate's chin and calls for a barber. The "barber" lathers the candidate, getting foam in his mouth. He

shaves him with what feels like a very, very rough blade. It's a shingle.

"Boxing Match"

Two candidates are selected for a boxing match. Belts are strapped around their waists. A six-foot rope connects the belts so that candidates do not wander blindly off. The boxers are given gloves. Unknown to the candidates, a member also puts on gloves and gives them occasional jabs from unexpected directions.

"Tug-of-War"

Two candidates or groups of candidates play tug-of-war. An unseen member sets the rope afire in the middle. It burns in two, and all fall down—on the electric carpet, if desired.

"The Thirst"

"This neophyte has asked for a drink of water," a member says. Another member replies that there is no water. "Then we must make water," says the first. Several members urinate in a bowl, making sure that the candidate hears. "It is ready," says a member. "Drink, and quench thy thirst." The candidate is handed a bowlful of warm water and forced to drink it.

"Punkin Pie"

This is just a forced pie-eating race, with the candidates' hands bound behind their backs. Other gustatory stunts involve making the blindfolded candidates eat various non- and quasi-edible materials: *Initiation Stunts* suggests ginger ale containing frankfurters and toilet-paper squares.

"The Shampoo"

A candidate is told that he must possess three essentials to be a member: keen vision, a sensitive touch, and an acute sense of smell. An egg is placed in his hand. "What is in your hand?" he is asked. The candidate replies, "An egg." "Correct. Now to test your sense of smell—is it a good egg or a bad egg?" The candidate answers. "We'll see if you are correct," the member says. He crushes an empty eggshell on the candidate's head and pours some water on it. He rubs the "egg" in the candidate's hair. Another member holds a bottle of ammonia or other evil-smelling substance under the candidate's nose.

"The Trained Dog"

A candidate is told that he must meet Fido, the trained dog. An authentic dog is brought in. "Fido snarls at neophytes and sometimes bites them in the calf of the leg," a member warns. Another pinches the candidate's leg. The dog is placed in the candidate's lap. The initiation ceremony proceeds with another candidate so that the first believes that attention has shifted from him. A member sneaks up on the candidate with the dog and trickles some warm water in his lap. He may also hold a smell bottle under the candidate's nose. "Naughty Fido!" all scold.

A variation is the "Bung Hole Test" a standard feature of Shriner initiations. No dog is required. Two blindfolded candidates are directed to opposite ends of a barrel or large metal cylinder lying on its side. They are told to crawl into the barrel or cylinder. The candidates bump heads in the middle. Outside, a lodge member yelps like a dog. Someone sprinkles warm water on the candidate's faces through a hole. A member yells, "Get that dog out of there! It just pissed in his face!"

"The Sacred Stone"

The candidate is told that a "sacred stone" is near his feet. He must make a sign of deference by bending over and placing his forehead as close to the ground as possible. When the candidate bends over, a member paddles him with a paddle containing an exploding cartridge. "The Little Rose" test is the same thing, only the candidate is told to pick a flower.

"The North Pole"

Candidates are forced to climb a greased pole while members paddle them. Afterward, a member hands a candidate a piece of ice: "Here is your share of the North Pole. Hold it as long as you can, and pass it on."

"Molten Lead Test"

A member warns the candidate that the next test may be dangerous if not performed carefully. Proof of a candidate's courage and faith in the order is required, the member explains. "Is the lead good and hot?" he asks another member. "Yes, red hot," he replies. "If you are not a coward, you must plunge your hands into a caldron of red-hot molten lead," the member tells the candidate. A large pot is set before the candidate. It contains any reasonably humane substitute for molten lead. If the candidate refuses to put his hands in the pot, the others force him.

"Good Rich Blood"

An overly "frisky" candidate is selected. "He has too much gall," a member says. "Then we must cut out his gall," another counters. A "doctor" is called for.

The candidate is forced onto a makeshift operating table. The doctor feels for the candidate's pulse. He pronounces the pulse too high. The doctor confers with other members. They decide that drawing a quart of "good rich blood" will make the patient less frisky.

The doctor pricks the candidate with a pencil point and dribbles warm water from a sponge on the wound. If there are other candidates present, a member says, moaning, "Stop! You're killing me!" Doctor and assistants demand "More blood"—"Go in deeper"—"Take some from the heart." The doctor presses a sharp piece of ice against the candidate's chest and draws the ice slowly across the chest. More warm water is dribbled. "He can't take much more of this"—"He's stopped breathing"—"He's dead." The doctor tells his assistants to take the body and throw it on the ash pit.

"The Test of Fire"

Candidates are told a club secret, say a secret number. A member later asks a candidate the secret number. The candidate answers as he has been told. "This infidel knows our secret number," objects the member. "He must not leave here alive. What is to be done with him?" Various tortures or means of execution are proposed: burning at the stake, cutting off the toes, burning out the eyes. The members soon agree on "The Test of Fire."

"You must be branded with the secret number," the blindfolded candidate is told. A fictitious red-hot branding iron is supplied. "Where should we brand him?" a member asks. "The most vital spot," another urges. One member "brands" the candidate's genitals with a warm piece of pipe or a sharp piece of ice while another scorches some raw meat with a candle flame under his nose. If there are other candidates waiting, a member screams. "He fainted," someone says. "Throw the body to the dogs."

"His Majesty, the King"

A candidate is accused of arrogance. "Let's crown him king, then," someone suggests. The candidate is taken to a "throne." This is a folded blanket suspended between two chairs. Lodge members sit on the chairs to hold the blanket in place. The candidate unknowingly sits on the blanket between the two chairs. Underneath the throne is a basinful of water. "Crown him," a member says. A spongeful of molasses is placed on the candidate's head and squeezed. The two members sitting on the blanket get up, dropping the candidate into the water.

"Hazing the Obstreperous"

Initiation Stunts offers the following remedy for unruly initiates: The offender is bound and taken to a special meeting place in the woods. He is securely blindfolded. One member forces him to the ground and holds his mouth open. The other members gather around and make coughing, gagging sounds. They plop a raw oyster into his mouth.

PART FIVE

Pay No Attention to the Man Behind the Curtain

L ose the TV Magic Cards. If you're like most jaded postteens, you don't care about the dinky little card and coin tricks explained in any of the hundreds of magic books for popular consumption. You just want to know how the bitchin' stuff works. How to saw a person in two. How to make a handkerchief dance in a sealed glass bottle. How to make Doug Henning's stage persona actually seem cute. It's fun to be fooled, sure. But it's even more fun to be able to point out the wires and mirrors and ruin it for everyone else.

Magicians get territorial when it comes to the primo material. But even the pros have to learn the secrets somewhere. The somewhere happens to be a handful of professional magic-materials suppliers, including Abbott's Magic Manufacturing Co. (Colon, MI 49040), Flosso Hornmann Magic Co. (304 West 34th Street, New York, NY 10018), U. F. Grant (P.O. Box 44052, Columbus, OH 43204), and Louis Tannen, Inc. (1540 Broadway, New York, NY 10036). All publish large catalogs advertising "workshop plans" for illusions. The plans—short, photocopied manuscripts—detail the secrets of the spectacular stage illusions and sell for a few dollars each. We sent away for some of the real bafflers. Promise you won't be disappointed afterward, and turn the page.

19·

David Copperfield's Dancing Handkerchief in a Bottle

Two of David Copperfield's best-known illusions are levitations of inanimate objects. One uses a large, metal-finish ball, which floats about the stage on command. At one point Copperfield passes the ball through his arms to demonstrate that no wires are used. The other effect, used in a TV commercial for Eastman Kodak, involves a knotted handkerchief. The handkerchief "dances" and jumps from hand to hand. When stuffed in a stoppered glass bottle, the handkerchief thrashes as vigorously as before. It "struggles" to get out and soon pops the stopper and jumps out.

Not only do both tricks seem to rule out all conventional means of support, but also the control of the floating objects is remarkable. Copperfield balances the seemingly heavy ball on a fingertip. It follows a slow, controlled arc to the other hand. The ball retreats from Copperfield, and then it comes back on command. The handkerchief becomes a puppetlike animation.

With cruder forms of levitation, it is a simple matter to decide who is controlling the object: the magician or an unseen flunky offstage. When the magician is in control, the object can strut like a marionette, but—surprise, surprise—it never strays more than an arm's length from the magician. As much of the audience gathers, the object *is* a marionette, just with extra-thin strings. When controlled offstage, the object can vary its distance from the performer and even rise above his head. But movements are slow and awkward. If moved too quickly, the object tends to develop a giveaway sway. Copperfield's method is so much more impressive that some postulate a novel technology—focused air currents or magnetic fields, say.

Copperfield is not the only magician to perform these illusions or variations of them. Mark Wilson first performed the floating-ball trick on national television. Doug Henning levitated an "enchanted silver sphere" in a 1982 TV special and a lighted candle in his Broadway musical, *Merlin*. Larry Wilson performs the dancing-handkerchief trick, with the handkerchief jumping in and out the doorways of a small wooden cabinet. In all cases, the method appears to be the same as Copperfield's.

The Floating Ball

The larger magic catalogs offer two illusions purporting to levitate a metallic ball. The simpler of the two is sold under the trade name Zombie. The Zombie illusion uses a lightweight, metal-finish ball with a secret hole. A cork fits snugly into the hole, and the cork is attached to one of the performer's fingers by a stiff wire. By moving the finger, the performer moves the ball. But the performer must always drape a cloth over or near the ball to hide the wire support. The ball may never vary its distance from the finger supporting it—and this distance is only about a foot.

With practice, the Zombie illusion is not as transparent as it may seem when described. It has the advantage of not requiring an elaborate setup. No amount of skill can conjure away the need for the cloth to conceal the wire support, however. Copperfield does not use a cloth with his floating ball.

The second illusion is described in "The Don Wayne Floating Ball," a manuscript sold by Louis Tannen, Inc. and other magic-materials suppliers. It is a far superior illusion to Zombie, and it is the method Copperfield uses—the manuscript acknowledges that Copperfield and Mark Wilson use it.

The ball is about eight inches across. It is hollow. It may be made of aluminum, acrylic, papier-mâché, or a lightweight plastic. In all cases, it weighs far less than its metal surface suggests.

Size A black silk thread suspends the ball. The average audience little appreciates how invisible a thread may be. For levitations of very small objects, magicians sometimes use a fine nylon that can be invisible at close range in full sunlight to a person of normal vision (they attach bits of adhesive wax to the ends so they will be able to work with it). Size A silk is visible from several yards, but this is remedied by careful choice of lighting and back-drop. If both the silk and the backdrop are black, the silk is very hard to see. The mirrored ball serves a double purpose. It makes the audience think that the ball is quite heavy and thus that any supporting threads would have to be good, thick, and visible. Also, the spotlight play on the ball's mirror surface blinds the audience to the dark threads.

(It doesn't always work that way. On "Doug Henning's Magic on Broadway," an NBC special broadcast November 14, 1982, the thread was visible several times—on home TV screens, yet—as Henning performed the illusion.)

An astute observer might notice that the ball's mobility is limited to a plane. As usually set up, the plane is parallel to the backdrop. It passes through, or just in front of the performer. The diagram shows why.

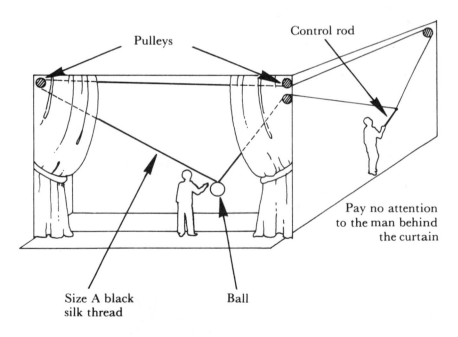

Pulleys

Control rod

Pay no attention
to the man behind
the curtain

Size A black
silk thread

Ball

The ball is supported by two threads coming from upper stage right and upper stage left. The two threads and ball actually are part of one continuous loop. At upper stage left, the thread passes over a pulley and then backtracks high over the performer to upper stage right. There it makes a ninety-degree turn over another pulley and passes over an offstage assistant to a pulley far offstage. There it angles down to the assistant, back up to a second pulley at upper stage right, and back to the ball.

Offstage, the thread is tied to an eyelet at the end of a rod held by the assistant. The motions of the eyelet in its plane correspond to the motions of the ball in its plane, with one difference: Vertical motions are reversed. Moving the eyelet up increases the slack in the thread and causes the ball to drop. Moving the eyelet down raises the ball. The ball-bearing pulleys ensure that the ball drops evenly and not from one side only. Horizontal motion of the eyelet moves the ball in the same direction.

The assistant is situated so that he can see the performer at all times. The backdrop may be partially transparent so the assistant can see the spotlighted performer and ball but the audience can't see the assistant in the shadows. Or ordinary curtains may block audience view of the assistant. Because the assistant is watching the performance in real time, he can control the ball almost as well as the performer himself could. Maneuvering the ball with the control rod becomes natural after a little practice. To make the ball jump from the performer's right hand to left hand (move from nine o'clock to three o'clock, clockwise, as seen from the audience), the assistant must swing the control rod eyelet in an arc from nine o'clock to three o'clock counterclockwise, as seen from far stage right.

The beauty of the trick is that no one expects threads to be diagonal. The magician can wave his hands above the ball, below it, and to either side. As far as most of the audience is concerned, this rules out the possibility of threads.

The ball cannot, of course, be passed completely through a fair vertical hoop. The illusion manuscript advises the performer to form his arms into a circle to one side of the ball, with the thread already passing through the arms. The ball can then be directed horizontally through the linked arms. Close observation of Copperfield and other performers shows that this is indeed what they do. If the performer wants to use a metal hoop, it must have a small break for the thread to pass through.

The Dancing Handkerchief

Small objects other than a ball may be levitated as well. Henning's burning candle seems to use the same setup as the floating ball. In principle, a handkerchief (perhaps containing a lead weight for stability) might be levitated in an identical manner. As performed by Copperfield, Larry Wilson, and others, however, the handkerchief trick has some additional features.

Occasionally the handkerchief is borrowed from an audience member. Even if the audience member is a confederate with a prethreaded handkerchief, the threads should be difficult to conceal from those sitting nearby.

Unlike the floating ball, the handkerchief frequently darts in and out of closed containers. It continues to move inside the containers.

The secret is to be found in another illusion manuscript, "Harry Blackstone's 'Spirit Dancing Handkerchief,'" available from Abbott's Magic Manufacturing Co. The illusion, including the routines with the glass bottle and the cabinet, was devised by Harry Blackstone (father of the Harry Blackstone, Jr., now performing). It requires two assistants.

At the beginning of the trick, a size "O" silk thread stretches across the stage at waist height. Each end is held by an offstage assistant.

The magician borrows an unprepared handkerchief from someone in the audience. Going back onstage, he ties a knot in the handkerchief—tying it around the thread. (The magician must turn his back to the audience as he does so, or the assistants must lower the thread briefly so that the magician can step over it and face the audience.)

The handkerchief is subsequently animated by the two assistants working in unison. The manuscript recommends red lights (to make the thread invisible) and a second thread lying on the floor in case the first one breaks.

The only preparation needed for the glass bottle is to shave about one-quarter to three-eighths inch from two opposite sides of the cork. After the handkerchief is placed in the bottle, the stopper must be aligned with the flat sides pointing to the assistants. This allows free space for the thread to slide smoothly over the glass. When inside the bottle, the handkerchief can jump up and down, but it must stay directly under the cork. The cork must, of course, fit very loosely for the handkerchief to pop it off.

The cabinet works the same way. Its edges must be rounded so the thread does not catch. The magician may stuff the handker-

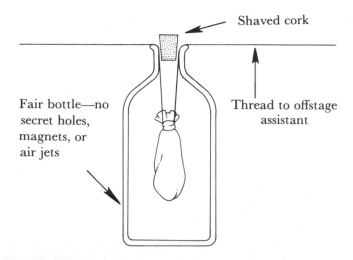

Shaved cork

Fair bottle—no secret holes, magnets, or air jets

Thread to offstage assistant

chief in one opening and pull it out through another. When the assistants then both pull on their ends of the thread, the handkerchief enters the cabinet through the latter opening, peeks out the first opening, and then jumps out.

At the end of the performance, the magician holds the handkerchief in one hand. One assistant lets go of his end of the thread. The other pulls. The thread slides through the handkerchief knot and is reeled in by the assistant. Meanwhile, the magician places his thumb behind the handkerchief knot and reanimates the handkerchief. It seems to be struggling to free itself. The magician walks out into the audience (which he couldn't do during the performance) and hands the handkerchief back to its owner.

20·

Harry Blackstone, Jr.'s
Sawing a Woman in Two

Harry Blackstone, Jr., performs the most spectacular of the sawing illusions: He saws through a woman, in plain view, with a
buzz saw. The saw looks and sounds real. It cuts through wood.
A woman lies down on a platform close to the blade. Unlike other
sawing illusions, no cabinet is used. The blade visibly slices
through the woman's torso, shredding part of her dress. Even
during the sawing, the head and legs move naturally. What
makes this illusion so baffling is that there seems to be no room for
deception. The audience sees everything, and what it sees is impossible.

Blackstone's buzz saw is, of course, a refinement of the basic
sawing-a-woman-in-two illusion. The sawing illusion has been
performed in various ways by various magicians ever since 1921.
Sexism, not anatomical constraints, dictates that a woman be
used. Horace Goldin, who pioneered the trick in the 1920s, originally used a male subject.

The Second-Woman Theory

Goldin's precise method is no matter of conjecture: He patented it
in 1923. If you write the U.S. Patent Office and request patent
number 1,458,575, they will send a complete description, including diagrams for construction of the cabinet.

A large, rectangular cabinet rests on a table. The cabinet may be lifted off the table and shown at various angles. The top of the cabinet unhinges. A woman gets into the cabinet, possibly assisted by audience volunteers. One end of the cabinet has three openings, for the woman's head and hands. The opposite end has two openings, for her feet. Once the woman's extremities are in place, the top of the cabinet is closed and padlocked. The cabinet may again be lifted to demonstrate that the woman is completely inside. The cabinet is replaced on the table, and the table is spun around to show the apparatus from all angles.

Using a large, genuine saw, the magician and an assistant cut through the cabinet at its center. The cabinet is usually presented to the audience lengthwise so that the woman's head, feet, and hands are visible at all times. If desired, audience volunteers may secure the woman's extremities during the sawing.

The saw is withdrawn. Two metal plates are fitted into preexisting slots just on either side of the cut. The two halves of the cabinet are pulled apart. The metal plates prevent the audience from seeing the (presumably bloody) results of the sawing. The magician points out the head, hands, and feet, which are still moving and obviously not fakes.

Then the two halves are shoved back into contact. The metal plates are removed, the padlocks are unlocked, and the top is opened. The woman steps out of the cabinet, uninjured and in one piece.

Goldin's trick uses two women. The second woman is hidden in the thickish tabletop on which the cabinet rests. Unknown to the audience, the bottom of the foot half of the cabinet has a pair of trapdoors that open upward only. The tabletop has a matching pair of doors. The two pairs of doors must be perfectly aligned. When the cabinet is lifted and replaced on the table, wood ridges on the tabletop help the magician position the cabinet correctly. As the magician spins the table, the feet point away from the audience for a moment. The first woman quickly pulls in her legs, resting her feet on a footrest built into the head half of the cabinet. This places the first woman entirely in the head half. The second woman opens the trapdoors and sticks her feet out the two openings in the end of the cabinet.

The box can then be sawed without harm. The metal plates prevent the audience from glimpsing the illusion's inner workings. Because of the trapdoors, only the head end can be moved.

Rejoining need take only a few seconds. The magician slides

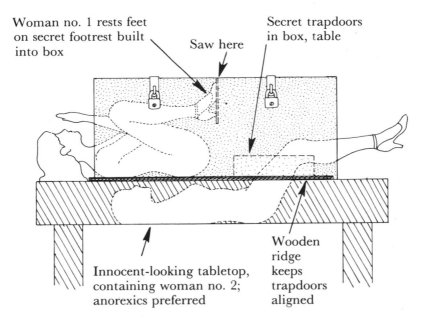

Woman no. 1 rests feet on secret footrest built into box

Saw here

Secret trapdoors in box, table

Innocent-looking tabletop, containing woman no. 2; anorexics preferred

Wooden ridge keeps trapdoors aligned

the head half back into place and removes the metal plates. One plate is casually propped against the cabinet in such a way as to block the audience's view of the feet. The two women switch feet as the magician unlocks the top of the cabinet.

An extra touch, created by Howard Thurston, has the magician snip off part of the woman's sock before the sawing. The magician pretends to hear a heckler protest that the feet are not real. "Spontaneously" he removes the woman's shoes, cuts off part of one sock, and asks an audience volunteer to testify that the foot is real. The second woman, of course, must wear a sock cut in the same manner. Thurston also had volunteers hold the woman's head and feet during the sawing. The person holding the feet was a confederate.

All modern magicians are haunted by the ghost of Goldin's second woman. Word of the second woman leaked out. Sophisticated audiences now expect there to be two women. In consequence, the two-woman method has become operationally extinct. (Abbott's Magic Manufacturing Co. sells a workshop plan for Thurston's method, but none of the well-known contemporary performers dares use it.) The voluminous cabinet and thick tabletop are passé. The modern sawing illusions are designed to banish any suspicion of a second woman.

The "Thin Model" Sawing

The method used by Doug Henning in *Merlin* comes closer to the ideal of a visible sawing. A cabinet is still used, but it is a thin cabinet (about twelve inches thick vs. more than eighteen inches for the old method). Skeptics must concede that even a contortionist cannot draw her knees up under her chin in a foot of crawl space. With the Goldin/Thurston method, the tabletop had to be thick as well. Henning's tabletop is about two inches thick.

The basic scenario is the same, with one innovation: two small doors in the front of the two halves of the cabinet. These may be opened to show the audience the cabinet interior. The cabinet top is opened, and the woman gets in. Stocks secure the head and feet (the arms are inside the cabinet). The two side doors are opened to show that the woman is indeed in the cabinet. The door in the head half shows the woman's arm and torso; the door in the foot half reveals her legs. The woman may stick her arm through the doorway and wave to the audience. The feet move as well. The doors are closed.

The cabinet is sawed through its center. Two metal plates go on either side of the cut. (In Henning's performance, the plate in the head end fails to go down all the way. Henning pulls on the woman's head, and the plate falls into place.) The two halves can then be separated. (The table is in two parts, each with three legs.) The halves may be shown from all angles.

The climax comes when the side doors of the disconnected halves are again opened. The woman's body is seen to be in the same position. Even a spectator thoroughly familiar with the Goldin/Thurston method is likely to conclude that the cabinet affords no room for a second woman and no room for the woman to scrunch up her body in some position other than where it seems to be.

The only thing suspicious about the setup is the triangular arrangement of the table legs. After all, everyone knows about those triangular tables with mirrors between the legs. But this suspicion doesn't pan out. When Henning or an assistant stands behind one of the table halves, their legs are visible underneath it. There are no mirrors.

In due course, the halves are reassembled, and the woman emerges whole. (In *Merlin*, Henning sawed two women in half and interchanged their halves.)

Henning's secret is revealed in a workshop plan titled "Thin Model Sawing A Woman In Half" and available from Louis Tannen, Inc. Henning's use of the "Thin Model" method is mentioned in the plan. Only one woman is used. In brief, the gimmicks are fake feet and a cabinet that is wide enough for the woman to pull up her knees *sideways.*

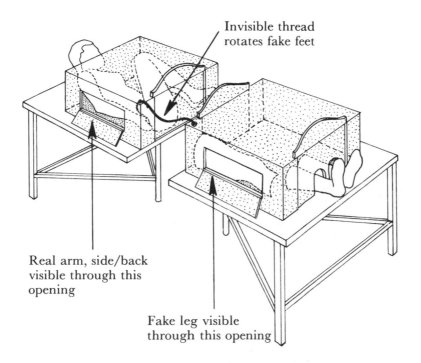

Invisible thread
rotates fake feet

Real arm, side/back
visible through this
opening

Fake leg visible
through this opening

According to the plan, the cabinet is 24½ inches wide. This allows just enough space for a slim woman to draw her legs up to her side. The legs are drawn up on the side away from the side door, of course. The woman's head remains facing upward.

The foot half of the cabinet is equipped with a set of mannequin feet. As soon as the woman gets in the cabinet, she draws herself up into the head half and pushes the fake feet through the opening at the foot end of the cabinet. (This action is in part concealed by the open doors on top of the cabinet.) The woman's real feet are never seen once she gets in the cabinet. The audience sees two feet emerge from the end of the cabinet and assumes them to be the woman's.

The feet must move to be convincing. They have two degrees of freedom. A slide mechanism with a leather grip lets the woman control the in-and-out motion (while the two halves of the cabinet are together). The feet are also on hinges that allow them to rotate inward and outward. This motion is controlled by an invisible monofilament thread operated by the woman or an offstage assistant. A spring attached to the hinges provides a restoring force to counter the string. From a distance, these two motions are sufficient—unless a heckler asks the woman to wiggle her toes.

The open side doors provide but a limited view of the interior. In the head section, you see a genuine arm. Behind it is the woman's costume covering what you take to be her side. Actually, it's the woman's back. The leg in the other side doorway is a built-in fake. It conceals the rotating feet mechanism.

For Henning's *shtick* with the metal plate, the woman evidently blocks the blunt plate with a hand or her feet until the right moment.

The Buzz Saw Illusion

Could fake legs likewise explain Blackstone's buzz saw illusion? The main objection is that there seems to be no opportunity to switch the real legs for the fakes. The woman lies down in full view. The legs are never out of sight. The same is true for the head.

The real secret, as explained in Abbott's "Buzz Saw Illusion" manuscript, is more ingenious yet. Both the head and legs are real. What is fake is the body. In effect, the buzz saw illusion uses a "cabinet" that is shaped like the woman's torso.

The illusion's wood structure incorporates a buzz saw and a mobile table. By means of a crank, the table can be moved under and past the blade of the stationary saw. The table surface hides a large rectangular depression (about 28⅞ inches long by 13½ inches wide by 7¼ inches deep). But the table is just about at audience eye level, so the depression is not noticeable.

As a preliminary demonstration, a strip of wood is secured to the table with a metal holder. The wood and holder bridges the hollowed-out part of the table. Unknown to the audience, the wood has been precut most of the way through. The uncut side is up. The buzz saw is switched on, and the table is drawn under the blade. When the wood is removed, it breaks easily in two.

Under her dress, the woman wears a strip-metal framework conforming to the back of her torso. This is secured with snaps on the abdomen side. The framework includes a strip of flesh-colored cardboard near the intended site of the cut.

As the woman lies down on the table, the billows of her dress—and a conveniently placed assistant—prevent the audience from seeing what is going on. The woman unsnaps the framework. Her midsection sags into the hollow. The framework, held in place by projections, seems to rest on a flat table.

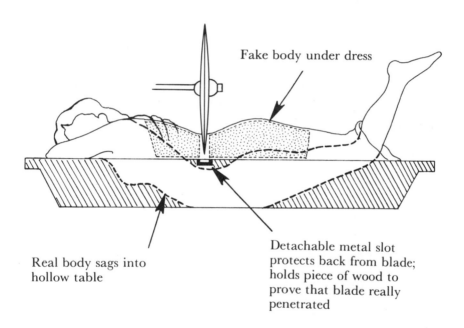

Fake body under dress

Real body sags into
hollow table

Detachable metal slot
protects back from blade;
holds piece of wood to
prove that blade really
penetrated

As a safety measure, the magician and his assistant reinsert the metal holder and a new wood strip "under" the woman's body. Ostensibly this is so the wood will be sawn in two and can be offered as evidence of penetration. Actually, the wood and metal holder go just over the woman's back, through a slot in the torso framework. The wood and metal thus protect the woman's back from the blade.

The swayback position is awkward but safe. Because the fake

body is cloaked in the dress, it does not have to be as well crafted as the fake legs in the "Thin Model" sawing illusion. By and large, audience suspicion is directed to the head and legs, which are genuine. The pink cardboard "back" does not bear close examination, but it is covered up with a cape as soon as the blade is clear. The Abbott's plan recommends dim lighting and a red spotlight on the woman.

If there is any danger to the illusion, it is incidental. The plan warns to take care that the woman's hair does not get caught in the belt driving the blade. The woman must keep her legs vertical, lest they come too close to the blade. The saw is of low power (three-quarter horsepower is suggested). It cuts a dress and pink cardboard but goes through wood with difficulty.

21·

Uri Geller's Blindfold Drive

Uri Geller has, in effect, been blacklisted from national television since talk-show hosts realized his feats were accomplished by trickery. After all, Geller's best-known effects are nontricks—tricks so unspectacular that no avowed magician would bother with them. Seeing a spoon bent or a watch started is exciting only if you believe Geller's claims of some weird supernatural power. Once you know it's a trick, it is easy to figure out.

Geller nonetheless continues to draw crowds of believers to his lectures/demonstrations. And not all of his effects are as easy to explain away as those bent spoons.

His demonstrations include "telepathy." An audience volunteer writes the name of a city or of a color on a blackboard, well out of sight of Geller. Geller correctly identifies the volunteer's choice.

Geller produces ten identical aluminum film cans. A volunteer secretly fills one of the cans with water and reseals it. The ten cans are placed in front of Geller. Without ever touching the cans, he successively eliminates those without water by pointing at them. The last can is found to be the one with the water. (This is one of the tricks that Johnny Carson, a former magician, foiled by keeping a guard on the test materials prior to a Geller *Tonight Show* appearance. Had Geller been a real psychic, Carson's precautions should not have made a difference.)

Geller claims offstage miracles as well. While eating lunch with astronaut Edgar Mitchell, Geller "materialized" a strange piece of metal in a mouthful of vanilla ice cream. Later the same day, another piece of metal materialized out of thin air. When the two pieces were put together, Mitchell recognized them as a tiepin he had lost years earlier.

From the standpoint of conventional magic, the best of Geller's tricks is a blindfold drive sometimes performed as a publicity stunt. Geller is securely blindfolded and then drives a car through city streets. He claims that he sees his way telepathically through the eyes of his passengers.

Geller is not the only performer to do the trick. The Astonishing Neil, another quasipsychic, put on an elaborate, televised version of the stunt for a *Real People* segment. Neil molded a thick layer of clay over his eyes, then blindfolded himself, and then tied a black hood over his head. He was taken to a town he had never been in before and given a map he had never seen before. He drove at moderate speed thus blindfolded, following the directions with the map. He also drove at high speed through a parking lot, managing not to hit volunteers standing at random points in the lot.

In 1975 magician James Randi (The Amazing Randi) wrote an exposé of Geller, *The Magic of Uri Geller* (New York: Ballantine Books), in which Randi insisted that the blindfold drive, as all of Geller's stunts, was done without psychic help. Being a magician himself, however, Randi did not tell how the trick is done.

Everybody Needs Friends

Part of Geller's secret is two friends who hide themselves in the audience during performances. For much of Geller's "telepathy," the entire audience sees the word being transmitted. Geller's accomplices are thought to signal to him.

Shipi Shtrang is a male Israeli several years younger than Geller. Shtrang has dark, wavy hair and looks like he could be Geller's younger brother. Shtrang stays out of the spotlight. He is rarely photographed—though a picture appears in Uri Geller's *My Story* (New York: Praeger, 1975). Geller met Shtrang when Geller was his counselor at a children's camp. The two collaborated on what seems to have been a basic vaudeville mind-reading act ("What is the woman holding up? *Watch* you don't miss it!"), playing small Israeli nightclubs. Leaving Israel, they classed up the act by claiming that Geller has real psychic powers. Shtrang may have helped Geller through his Stanford Research Institute tests by signaling answers.

Geller's other confederate, Solveig Clark, is an attractive, blond, American woman. According to David Marks, a psychologist at the University of Otago in New Zealand who observed Geller during a New Zealand tour, Clark frequently sits in an unoccupied section of the theater, in clear view of Geller. When an audience volunteer writes the name of a color on a chalkboard, Clark relays the name of the color to Geller with hand signals. Geller counts "one, two, three"; the "three" is Clark's cue to signal. Marks identified two of the signals: Waving the hands up and down while the wrists rest on top of the seat in front means "blue." When Clark folds her arms and pats her upper left arm with her right hand, it's "purple."

The Film Cans

There are several ways to do the trick with the ten sealed film cans. Geller eliminates the cans one by one, ending up with the one containing water. The magicians who have exposed the trick seem not to be sure which method Geller uses, but plainly there is little reason to assume clairvoyance. In brief, Geller could (a) breathe on the cans to see which one collects dew; (b) bump the table to see which can moves less; (c) check the adhesive tape around the lids for signs of resealing (before the subject fills one of the cans, Geller could make sure that all cans have a small, precise amount of overlap of the ends of the tape); or (d), the quick and dirty approach, shake the cans during a moment when no one is around.

The Tiepin Miracle

The simplest and most convincing analysis of Geller's offstage miracles credits simple, bold cheating. Geller somehow got hold of a "lost" tiepin of Mitchell's. (Martin Gardner has suggested Geller looked under the seats of Mitchell's car.) Geller broke the pin in two, then popped one piece into his mouth while coughing at lunch. Later he tossed the other piece in the air when no one was looking.

The Blindfold Drive

The blindfold drive is explained in "Sightless Vision," a manuscript that is sold, complete with hood, by Louis Tannen, Inc. The full "Sightless Vision" routine is too slick for Geller's purposes (Geller must take care that his tricks don't look like magic tricks), but the method seems certain to be the same.

The "Sightless Vision" performer produces an assortment of blindfolding gear: a handkerchief, aluminum foil, cotton balls, masking tape, powder puffs, bread dough, cardboard, and a black hood. Audience volunteers are invited to inspect the material. All are indeed found to be opaque. The volunteers assist in blind-folding the performer. A cardboard mask goes over the eyes, then lumps of dough, then silver dollars, and so forth. This material is held in place by wrapping gauze around the head and taping. Then the black hood goes over the head and is tied at the neck.

The performer is able to describe the dress of audience members. He can name objects they hold up. A plank may be placed across two supports, and audience volunteers can place their watches on the plank. The performer can walk the plank without stepping on the watches or falling off. And, of course, the performer can drive a car safely through city streets.

At the end of the demonstration, the sundry layers of the blindfold are ceremoniously removed. All are intact.

There is no way the performer could do all that he does unless he is able to see reasonably well while blindfolded. The trick is to make sure that the gauze or handkerchief is not tied too tightly. Although audience members help in fixing the gauze, they rarely pull it tightly for fear of hurting the performer. As the performer pulls the hood down over his head, he shoves the gauze, dough, cardboard, etc., down just enough to see over them.

Part of the hood is of single-thickness cloth. (When the performer demonstrates the hood to an audience member, he makes sure the opaque part goes over the eyes.) By looking over the gauze/dough assembly and through the thin part of the hood, the performer has serviceable vision. He must hitch up the gauze before removing the hood.

Geller's blindfold is less elaborate, but there can be little doubt that he can see through his blindfold, too. A single thickness of an ordinary silk handkerchief is reasonably transparent when pulled tight close to the eyes. Two thicknesses are nearly opaque. Geller only has to fold a handkerchief so that a crack of single-thickness silk is left to see through.

22·

Doug Henning's
Vanishing Horse and Rider

A faked accident draws gasps at the climax of this illusion. As performed in *Merlin,* Doug Henning rides a small horse into a cratelike structure. (On television, Henning has used a motorcycle.) Initially, the front of the wood structure is open so that the audience can see both Henning and the horse. Four heavy chains slowly raise the structure from the floor of the stage. Henning and the horse are still visible, and the crate is isolated from the floor, the sides of the stage, the backdrop, and the ceiling. There seems to be nowhere for Henning and the horse to go. Then the crate—which looked rickety all along—suddenly collapses. A horse's muffled whinny is heard—but Henning and the horse have vanished. Only the edges of the crate remain in place; the bottom and back sides dangle below.

A second or two later, Henning and the horse (or motorcycle) are revealed safe in a distant part of the stage or in a separate, suspended frame. The audience is left wondering not only how the trick was done but also how the horse was trained to perform whatever moves may be required of it.

Vanishing Techniques

There are only three basic ways to make a person vanish. One is to lower the person through a trapdoor in the stage. The second is to conceal the person with a judicious placement of mirrors. The third is to conceal the person behind a panel or curtain that blends into the background. Henning uses all three methods in his repertoire of illusions.

At another point in *Merlin,* for instance, Henning sits in a simple chair, well away from the backdrop and sides of the stage. A blue cloth is draped over Henning and the chair. A few seconds later, the cloth is snatched away. Henning is gone. (The chair is still there.) Henning then reappears from another part of the stage.

This effect appears identical to a very old illusion using a trapdoor under the chair. A wire frame maintains the shape of the body in the chair as the performer drops through the seat of the chair (it's on a hinge) and a trapdoor beneath. The wire frame is drawn away with the cloth.

Use of mirrors was apparent on "Doug Henning's Magic on Broadway" TV special. Henning made a woman and a million dollars appear and disappear from a transparent cubical box. The box rested on what appeared to be a simple four-legged table. For each appearance and disappearance, the box was covered with an opaque screen.

Anyone familiar with magic would have suspected an "Owens table"—a table with vertical mirrors running between the legs. The mirrors reflect the floor or carpet so that it looks as if you are seeing the carpet under and behind the table. Actually, there is a secret space between the mirrors. The woman and the money could have been hidden in this space to effect a disappearance.

The trouble with the Owens table is that the mirrors must be aligned just right for the perspective of the audience (or TV camera). In at least one camera shot of Henning's special, the mirrors were noticeably out of alignment. The reflection of the floor was a little higher than the floor itself. This was particularly evident if you looked at the line where the floor met the backdrop. It zigzagged as it went "behind" the legs of the table.

The third method is the simplest, but its use is limited. With suitable misdirection, a person may be hidden behind a panel matching the background. This is just the large-scale version of the false bottom in a magician's hat. Usually, the edges of the panel must be concealed. Dark colors, dim lighting, and a distant audience are preferred.

Two Horses, a Henning Look-Alike

If you give the horse-and-rider illusion some thought, you'll realize that there have to be two horses and two riders. The fake Henning has to be the first one, the one who vanishes. Before the illusion, no one expects a substitution. Henning has opportunity to duck offstage and send in his double. The Henning who reappears, however, has to stand up to the scrutiny of a suspicious audience.

The double used in *Merlin* is no dead ringer for Henning. As the crate is being raised, he looks away from the audience and waves, raising his arm so that it blocks his face.

Granting the switch, we are still left with an impressive illusion. The rider, who as it happens is not Henning, and the horse, which is alive, genuine, and heavy, both suddenly disappear far above the stage floor. The illusion is again an old one. It was devised by Clayton L. Jacobsen, who called it the "Vanishing Motorcycle and Rider" and explained it in *The Seven Circles*, a magazine for magicians. The idea of using a horse instead of a motorcycle was likewise Jacobsen's.

The crate must be sturdy. As the crate is being raised, the front is opened. The front is closed just before the disappearance. The bottom of the crate is equipped with a movable shelf that slides out toward the back (away from the audience). In fact, there is no back to the crate, so horse and rider both slide back the instant they are out of the audience's sight. A roller curtain made of the same material as the backdrop is pulled down in front of the horse and rider.

Then the crate "collapses." Actually, the crate edges, the secret shelf, and the curtain remain. The horse and rider are both still up there, behind a curtain that is indistinguishable from the backdrop. (Or, in a variation of the method, the fake backdrop is stretched between two of the supporting chains. Horse and rider are lifted up and out of sight by means of cables and a harness.) The frightened-horse sound is probably a recording. All that either horse must do is stand still and not be frightened by the commotion.

If the audience looked at the crate long enough, they might suspect the false backdrop. But they don't. Before anyone quite realizes what has happened, the real Henning is revealed—and attention shifts to him.

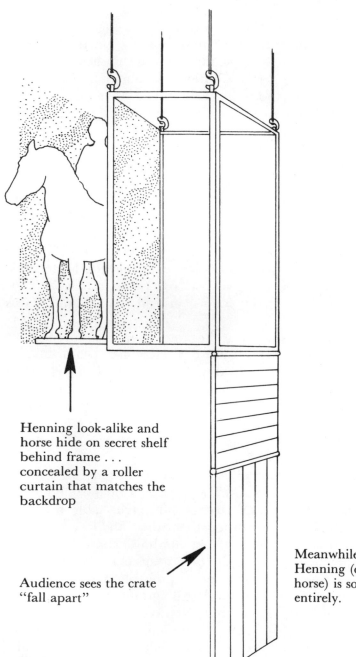

Henning look-alike and
horse hide on secret shelf
behind frame . . .
concealed by a roller
curtain that matches the
backdrop

Audience sees the crate
"fall apart"

Meanwhile, the real
Henning (on identical
horse) is somewhere else
entirely.

23·

The Amazing Kreskin's Social Security Number Divination

The Amazing Kreskin (a.k.a. George Kresge, Jr.) says he has extrasensory perception. Much of what Kreskin does is amazing, but nothing more so than his "telepathic" divination of audience Social Security numbers. Many millions of people have seen the trick on television, and it is one of the most difficult effects to explain. No other well-known magician seems to perform it. Magic catalogs do not sell a manuscript for it. The more gullible among Kreskin's audience readily swallow his claims of supernatural powers. The less gullible are driven to ridiculous extremes in attempting to explain the trickery.

Some think the audience subjects are accomplices. Some think Kreskin lip-reads from subjects who unconsciously mouth the digits while concentrating on their Social Security numbers. It has been suggested seriously that Kreskin plants hidden microphones or cameras in the theaters; that his Coke-bottle-thick glasses are a pair of telescope lenses; that he goes on a pickpocketing spree while mingling with the audience before the show. Or maybe he canvasses the parking lot, takes down license plate numbers, then phones the Department of Motor Vehicles to get the vehicle owners' Social Security numbers.

The intriguing thing about the trick is its apparent simplicity. Kreskin just concentrates on the number and gets it. Sometimes he writes the number on a board; sometimes he announces the digits in slow succession. Kreskin fumbles a lot, but he's rarely if ever wrong. He'll say: "I'm getting a 6, but I'm not sure it's the next digit"; "3-4-0, no, wait, maybe 3-5-0"; and so forth. He solicits minor help from the subject: "Is there a double digit?" "Just tell me, the next digit isn't a 4, is it? I think I'm getting a 4 from somebody else in the audience." But an occasional uh-huh or shake of the head can be of little consequence in selecting the correct nine-digit number out of a billion possibilities.

Sometimes an audience member is chosen before Kreskin starts reading his or her number. At other times, Kreskin starts announcing the digits of a number he is receiving, and then someone recognizes it as his number and stands up.

A few would-be explanations can be dismissed immediately. It is not, it seems, a necessary condition of the trick that the subjects take their Social Security cards out of their wallets. So Kreskin can't depend on spies to read the cards over the subjects' shoulders and signal the digits. Nor are the subjects themselves in cahoots with Kreskin. If you attend consecutive stage performances or videotape talk-show appearances, you'll note that the subjects are indeed different people every time. Unless Kreskin has a veritable army of accomplices, the subjects must be innocent audience members.

A Typical TV Performance

Kreskin's telepathy is not limited to Social Security numbers. In a typical performance, he reads names, dates, places, phone numbers, license plate numbers, and other personal information that he should have no way of knowing.

During an appearance on *The Mike Douglas Entertainment Hour* aired in February 1982, Kreskin scored five hits—and some misses (dialog approximate):

> KRESKIN: I'm getting the names "Chris" and "Elaine."
> (A man stands up.)
> SUBJECT 1: Chris and Elaine are my kids.
> KRESKIN: Do you have another child?
> SUBJECT 1: Yes.
> KRESKIN: Does the initial J mean anything to you?
> SUBJECT 1: Yes.
> KRESKIN: Joan?
> SUBJECT 1: Joan is my third child.
> (Man sits down.)
> KRESKIN: I'm getting something about a right shoulder. Is anyone having problems with a right shoulder? (Pause) I'm also getting the word "Jamaca."
> (Woman stands up.)

SUBJECT 2: That's the street where I live.

KRESKIN: I get something about a wedding ring, too. (Pause) Could you please concentrate on your Social Security number? Three . . . nine . . . three . . . seven . . . zero . . . four . . . seven . . . seven . . . six.

SUBJECT 2: That's correct.

(Woman sits down.)

KRESKIN: Institute of fashion, something about an institute of fashion. I'm getting Chicago, too.

(Woman stands up.)

KRESKIN: Are you from Chicago?

SUBJECT 3: That's right.

KRESKIN: Does institute of fashion mean anything to you?

SUBJECT 3: Not really. I'm going to college . . .

KRESKIN: Does the college have anything to do with fashion?

SUBJECT 3: No.

KRESKIN: But I do get that you're thinking of your favorite actor. Is that correct?

SUBJECT 3: Yes.

KRESKIN: I'm getting . . . Cary Grant.

SUBJECT 3: Right.

(Woman sits down.)

KRESKIN: I'm getting the name "Colleen," or maybe it's "Maureen." (Pause) Someone here had a flat tire last Thursday night.

(Man stands up.)

SUBJECT 4: I did.

KRESKIN: You had a flat tire?

SUBJECT 4: Yes.

KRESKIN: And it was last Thursday night?

SUBJECT 4: Yes.

KRESKIN: Does Colleen or Maureen mean anything to you?

SUBJECT 4: No.

(Man sits down.)

KRESKIN: Golden . . . the word "golden" . . . I'm getting Colorado, it's the town of Golden, Colorado. (Pause) I get skiing . . .

(Man stands up.)

SUBJECT 5: Yes.

KRESKIN: What does Golden, Colorado, mean to you?

SUBJECT 5: I just went skiing there.

KRESKIN: Does the year 1979 mean anything to you?

SUBJECT 5: I was married in 1979.
(Man sits down.)
KRESKIN: Has someone here lost a bracelet? Or found a lost bracelet?
(No one acknowledges it.)

Kreskin's mind reading is far from perfect, but he's right about a lot of things that could not have been lucky guesses.

Does Kreskin Have ESP?

According to Kreskin, it's all perfectly paranormal. He defends his claims of ESP in an autobiography, *The Amazing World of Kreskin* (New York: Random House, 1973):

> ... I do pick up information through a kind of telepathy. By deep concentration, "tuning in," I seek out and then "receive" a single thought, provided the "sender" is concentrating to an almost equal depth. Some debunkers have claimed it is an ability to "muscle read" a subject's face, to decipher clues given unconsciously by the subject. This may well be a factor of ESP, as natural as an eye blink, but I am not aware of it. The reaction on the subject's face may unconsciously increase my perception of the thought, but it does not reveal the thought unless an absolute "yes" or "no" answer is involved. Anyone can usually read a positive or negative simply by studying eye register.
>
> More than all this, if I perceive a Social Security number secreted in a purse at two hundred feet in a darkened theater, muscle reaction is of little help in determining the numbers and their sequence. The only source is the subject's concentration. His or her face, at that distance, is but a small shadowy object. ... I don't have the talents to see through the cloth of a lady's purse or through the leather of a man's wallet, wherein usually lies the small card on which the Social Security number is imprinted. So the only possible method is to read it with and through the mind of the cooperating sitting or standing subject. On receiving his or her signal, I project the numbers, visualizing them almost instantly. "The number is 225-12-6018." ... So while talking to an audience, I'm constantly writing, although I'm not really aware of the pencil movement. The material is usually ahead of what I'm trying to say to the audience or receive from them. ... I do not always look at what the pencil has written on my note pad. *225-12-6018.* I am not always confident it will be cor-

rect. Most of the time, though, the written number will match the verbal projection.

Yet Kreskin admits to using ordinary magician's sleight of hand in other parts of his act. His stage act includes conventional magic (card tricks and the like) and a comic hypnosis routine as well as the mind-reading feats.

How Kreskin Does It

The most comprehensive analysis of Kreskin's mind reading is to be found in *The Psychology of the Psychic* by David Marks and Richard Kammann, two New Zealand psychologists (Buffalo, N.Y.: Prometheus Books, 1980). Marks and Kammann attended a 1974 stage performance by Kreskin in Dunedin, New Zealand. After the show, they advertised in local newspapers for Kreskin's subjects. Interviews with the subjects who responded allowed Marks and Kammann to figure out how Kreskin did what he did.

Of course, the Social Security number trick is performed in the United States only. Marks and Kammann did not see it and thus did not cover it in their explication of Kreskin's techniques.

Big Secrets located one of Kreskin's American subjects. From his description of Kreskin's "mind reading," as well as Marks' and Kammann's analysis and Kreskin's televised performances, it is possible to deduce how Kreskin reads Social Security numbers. The trick is a gem of the magician's art. It uses misdirection, sleight of hand, and an entirely novel means of deception: the television talk show.

To understand how the trick works on television, let's first review Kreskin's stage act. Kreskin warms up his nightclub audience with some routine magic tricks and a few "experiments" to test the audience's vibes. Two examples of the latter:

1. "I am thinking of two simple geometric shapes, one inside the other," says Kreskin. "Concentrate, try to receive my thoughts, and project them on your mental screen."
2. "I'm thinking of a number between 1 and 50. Both digits are odd, but they aren't the same odd digit—15 would be okay, but not 11. Try to project the number on your mental screen."

(Do you have ESP? Draw the two shapes and write the number on a sheet of paper. Then turn to page 179.)

Next comes the mind reading. Kreskin invites the audience to write down any thoughts they want to send. He goes into the audience, dispensing paper, pencils, and envelopes. During the five minutes or so it takes to distribute materials and write messages, Kreskin jokes with audience members or fills up the time with patter about ESP. Then Kreskin instructs the audience to fold their completed messages and place them in envelopes (Marks' and Kammann's subjects) or to throw their messages on the floor (*Big Secrets'* subject). When the envelopes are used, they are given to audience members at the ends of rows for safekeeping. This done, the mind reading begins.

At the performance Marks and Kammann witnessed, Kreskin later went back into the audience, carrying his clipboard (the one he uses to write some of his predictions). He asked some of the people holding the envelopes to take a few folded messages and place them on his clipboard. Kreskin emphasized the fact that he did not so much as touch the slips of paper. Using the clipboard as a tray for the messages, Kreskin returned to the stage, sat down, and placed the clipboard beside him. He explained that he was going to try an experiment in thought transmission. Three volunteers were selected. Each took a message from the clipboard and (per Kreskin's instructions) read it, memorized it, and tore it up. One by one the volunteers concentrated on their messages. Each time, Kreskin divined the messages word for word. The rest of the audience had to take the volunteer's word for the accuracy of Kreskin's mind reading, though.

There is more to Kreskin's stage act, but the foregoing segments are the ones that bear on Kreskin's method for reading Social Security numbers. To the audience, it may seem that Kreskin uses the same technique, whatever it may be, throughout the mind-reading part of his act. In fact, there is reason to believe that Kreskin uses four or more distinct methods.

Let's start with the simplest. Many of Kreskin's readings work by nothing more than well-calculated luck. Take the following hypothetical exchange:

KRESKIN: Does the date September 11 mean anything special to anyone?
SUBJECT: Yes.
KRESKIN: Is it a birthday, an anniversary?
SUBJECT: It's my daughter's anniversary.

KRESKIN: I see something about your daughter and an automobile.
SUBJECT: She just bought a car.

Now think about it. There are hundreds of people in the audience. Everyone has a birthday. Most people have other special days. No matter what date Kreskin names, it is almost certain to draw a response.

Once someone claims September 11, Kreskin goes for a second match. This time he has to play it safe because he already has his subject. The subject admitted a daughter, so Kreskin sees something about the daughter and an automobile. Again, almost everyone can think of "something about an automobile." Kreskin is vague and lets the subject fill in the details. He knows that much of the audience will soon forget who said what first. Many will go home honestly believing that Kreskin divined the date of a subject's daughter's anniversary and the fact that she had purchased a car.

As it happened, Kreskin's luck was bad on the *Mike Douglas* guest shot mentioned above. Out of five or six attempts at a lucky coincidence, five fell flat. "Right shoulder," "wedding ring," "institute of fashion," "Colleen or Maureen," and "lost bracelet" all seem to have been guesses; "1979" may have been. The trick is to select associations rare enough to astonish those who claim them and yet common enough to make a coincidence likely. Perhaps Kreskin tailors his predictions to the size of the audience, going for more offbeat associations when the house is large. In any case, Kreskin has learned to recognize a dead end and wastes no time moving to another prediction when one fails.

Kreskin's second technique apparently is to steal a few of the messages he has his audience write. *Big Secrets'* informant noted that Kreskin "mind-read" the very same messages his party had written and thrown on the floor. Marks and Kammann say they actually saw Kreskin palm messages and put them in his pocket.

Most of the audience assumes that all the messages are still on the floor or in the envelopes. So they don't necessarily think it suspicious when Kreskin mind-reads the same thoughts they wrote down. Kreskin has told them to write the thoughts they want to transmit. Even if a subject is not concentrating on the same message during the mind reading, his thoughts can hardly help but return to his original message once Kreskin announces a key word of it. The subject *will* be thinking of his written message as Kreskin hems and haws, revealing it bit by bit.

Kreskin scribbles on his note pad a lot, and maybe he uses it as a scratch sheet. It probably isn't always convenient to reveal a palmed message right after looking at it. Kreskin may save himself the trouble of remembering complex messages by writing them on his board.

Speaking of the writing board, Marks and Kammann suspect that it is a "magician's tray"—a standard prop with two bottoms, allowing a quick switch of written messages.

The board looks a little funny. It has two flaps that allow Kreskin to use it as a tray for his "thought transference experiment" messages. But Kreskin does his best to allay suspicion. He uses the board for his notes all along, and he explains that he uses it for the written messages only to demonstrate that he does not touch the messages.

Could Kreskin steal a glance at the messages while they are in the tray? Maybe . . . many people fold their messages only once. If Kreskin is quick enough, he might glimpse a word or two while maintaining his patter and eye contact. But it takes more than that to explain Kreskin's accuracy. Despite his usual false starts, Kreskin reveals the messages verbatim. His accuracy in the thought-transference experiment seems much higher than in his general mind reading.

Marks and Kammann note that Kreskin always sets his tray/writing board down on the stage before proceeding. The flaps fold when the board is set down. When Kreskin picks the board back up, he apparently opens it to a second bottom containing a set of prepared messages. The prepared messages would be written by Kreskin and memorized before the show. Kreskin could get away with this because of the way the thought-transference experiment is set up. The people concentrating on the messages are not the people who wrote them but an arbitrary set of volunteers (often people in the front row). The volunteers have no way of knowing if the messages are fakes. Neither does the rest of the audience.

Kreskin does not ask for the original authors of these messages to reveal themselves. Marks' and Kammann's series of newspaper ads located eight of eleven visible audience participants from the

Kreskin performance they attended. But they failed to locate a single person who had written a message used in the thought-transference experiment. (They located all three of the volunteers who concentrated on the messages.) The most natural conclusion is that no one wrote the messages—no one other than Kreskin himself.

Kreskin may use still a fourth technique. In his biography, Kreskin says that he takes a long walk before every performance to improve his concentration. If so, he could easily manage a detour through the theater or studio parking lot. He could note license plate numbers and makes of cars. (Describing cars often is part of Kreskin's act.) Or better yet, Kreskin may look for bumper stickers and personal articles inside cars. Say Kreskin spots a car with a Missouri license plate, a racquetball sticker, and a child's toy and a Szechuan cookbook in the back seat. It isn't hard to imagine how he could weave this information into a fantastic demonstration of "mind reading."

By mixing these different techniques, Kreskin throws skeptics off the track. An explanation that works for one reading can't work for others. Kreskin mixes techniques even with a single subject. He may read the name of a subject's hometown (from a palmed written message) and then ask if he or she is thinking about a relative (a likely guess). Kreskin probably resorts to occasional ad hoc tricks, too. During a performance, Kreskin once mentioned that he had the feeling someone was wondering what happened to the rest of a twenty-dollar bill. A shocked waitress almost dropped her tray, Kreskin claims. She had just found half of a twenty-dollar bill on the floor, minutes earlier. It isn't hard to guess who lost it.

The Magic of Television

Back to the Social Security number trick. Of the millions who have seen the trick, it is significant that only a slim minority have seen it in person. The rest have seen it only on TV. It's a safe bet that most of those who have seen it live first saw it on TV. The public conception of what the trick is and how Kreskin performs it is derived almost entirely from TV.

That shouldn't make a difference, but it does. Granted, there is a long tradition, going back to the infancy of television, that no camera trickery is used in televised magic, that "you are seeing exactly what the studio audience is seeing." Kreskin, however, has devised the best camera trick of all—that of having the cameras turned off during a part of the Social Security number trick that is essential to understanding how the trick is done. It isn't that Mike, Merv, and Johnny are in on the trick. But Kreskin is aware of the time constraints of a TV talk show and has discovered how to use them to his advantage.

Which of his techniques does Kreskin use for Social Security numbers? A lucky guess is out. So are switched messages—Kreskin reads the numbers of people who stand up for everyone to see. Nothing Kreskin sees in the parking lot is likely to help him, either. That leaves the stolen-message technique.

The only necessary assumption is that some audience members write down their Social Security numbers as a message. Given Kreskin's reputation for reading Social Security numbers, this is an obvious choice. It takes no imagination; it's unique—no one else has the same Social Security number; yet for the shy, it's not too personal. If need be, Kreskin can hint that a Social Security number would be okay as a message.

The farther removed you are from Kreskin's "mind reading," the better it looks. Kreskin's subjects know they wrote the messages Kreskin reads. If they are of a skeptical turn of mind, they must suspect trickery. Nonsubject audience members know the entire audience wrote messages beforehand—but they probably attach little importance to it. Kreskin's TV audience is even more at a loss.

Obviously, Kreskin can't do his whole act on TV. What you usually see is this: The host introduces Kreskin, they chat briefly, and Kreskin goes right into his mind reading. He reads Social Security numbers, names, addresses, license plates, and other personal information, much of which couldn't be a lucky guess.

What you *don't* see is Kreskin passing out slips of paper for written messages, just as in the stage act. He may do this before the taping begins, in a commercial break, or within the sequence of the show if the tape will be edited for broadcast.

Kreskin explains the messages as a means of preparing the audience for telepathy and improving his rapport. Kreskin makes sure it takes several minutes to distribute paper, write messages, and collect them—dull, boring minutes in which nothing is happening; bad television. A tightly scheduled talk show cannot possibly allow five or ten minutes of what amounts to dead air. (An entire guest segment may be less than ten minutes.) So the host and producer see nothing wrong with handling Kreskin's preliminaries off-camera.

The omission is crucial. To the studio audience, Kreskin's Social Security number trick is pretty good. But to the home TV audience, which never suspects the written messages, it is incredible and seamless—a trick so inexplicable that many are prepared to believe it is no mere trick at all.

Finding the Paycheck

Kreskin does another trick that seems beyond the realm of ordinary prestidigitation. Near the end of each stage show, he locates his hidden paycheck "telepathically."

While Kreskin is offstage, a team of about four persons hides the paycheck. They are permitted to hide the check anywhere in the theater. It need not be in plain sight. After Kreskin returns, he warns the audience not to do or say anything to give the hiding place away. Kreskin wanders the theater with the team of hiders, looking for the check. Usually Kreskin holds one end of a handkerchief, and a hider holds the other end as Kreskin searches.

Kreskin is remarkably accurate. He forefeits his check (it goes to a charity of his choosing, actually) if he fails to find it. This has happened three times. Kreskin almost always finds the check before people start to get bored. He is expected actually to produce the check: If, say, it is hidden in a woman's purse, he must not only find the right woman but also ask her to open her purse and find the check inside.

Kreskin has a standing offer of twenty thousand dollars to anyone who can prove that he uses confederates in this trick. Moreover, the hiders are typically people known to many members of the audience—local celebrities, such as mayors, police chiefs, casino executives—so that complicity will not be suspected.

If Kreskin seems paranoid on this point, it's because the trick would be very easy to perform with a confederate. Everyone in the audience sees where the check is hidden, so a plant could direct Kreskin with a few discreet signals.

Most likely, the trick is legitimate. Kreskin probably does it by skillfully observing the reactions of the hiders and his audience. As in some of his mind-reading tricks, there's safety in numbers. Kreskin can count on there being a few people in every large audience who will give things away. They may keep glancing back to the hiding place or muttering to their neighbors when he makes a crucial turn. As to Kreskin's hiders, his admonitions not to show any reaction make it all the harder for them not to do so.

Other magicians can do cruder versions of this stunt; Kreskin is simply very good at it from years of practice. As he explains in his biography, he started as a child, playing the game of Hot and Cold:

> A player leaves the room and the rest of the class hides a bean bag. The player returns and begins to look for the bag, with the class shouting "Getting hotter" or "Getting colder." . . . Wouldn't it be great, I told my parents, if the object could be found without all the directions, just by having the "hiders" think about where it was? With the blessing of childhood, I didn't know the rules—what could be done, what couldn't. I tried it with my parents and had no success, naturally. They lost interest.
>
> But then I persuaded [my brother] Joe to try it. I literally forced him to practice with me for about four months. By the end of that time I could find almost any object in our small, cluttered room without him saying "hot" or "cold." I had no idea what I was doing, nor how much I was reading his facial expressions (a lot, probably) as I neared the object, but now I realize I was blindly beginning to train myself in sensitivity and ESP.

ESP? If Kreskin had it, he wouldn't need to palm messages for the mind reading. Kreskin's skill in finding his paycheck is remarkable, but there's no reason to assume it is anything supernatural.

Answers to ESP Test

Look at the opposite page. No ESP here. These tricks work because most people's minds work much the same way. No. 1? Figure that there are only three simple shapes (circle, square, triangle) that people are likely to think of. The most popular pair is the circle and triangle—no one knows why, but that's how it works out—and the civil defense symbol configuration is slightly

1. "A triangle in a circle—or the other way around."

2. "Thirty-seven. Actually, I was thinking of 35 first, but I changed my mind."

favored. As usual, Kreskin plays both sides of the street. No. 2? It sounds as if there are almost twenty-five numbers to choose from. Really there are only eight: 13, 15, 17, 19, 31, 35, 37, and 39. And hardly anyone picks 15 because Kreskin mentioned it. About a third of the population picks 37, and another quarter pick 35. Those that pick 35 are scarcely less impressed to hear that Kreskin rejected it.

The catch is, these tricks can't be done for the same audience twice. Kreskin doesn't repeat them when he has more than one show in a town. He can't ever do them on national television.

PART SIX

Always the Last to Know

You should have suspected that something important was being bumped when they started running Wishing Well and Jumble on the front page. But aren't all newspapers playing up features to compete with TV? A few weeks later, you can't remember either of your state's senators. You're living in a soft-news fantasy world—a world where nothing that happens in Washington or Beijing is ever more important than local high school basketball. A world called Knight-Ridder, Gannett, or Newhouse. Everyone said it couldn't happen in your town—until the day the capitalists took over the newspapers.

Soon there's a new managing editor—and a new slant to the lead photo captions ("The weatherman says fall doesn't arrive till 2:09 P.M. Friday, but try telling that to these little pixies ... the Molenar quads of 2491 Euclid Avenue.") There's an increased emphasis on TV listings, Erma Bombeck, and 4-H news (each in a separate four-color pullout). Then one day you wake up and realize you're reading the kind of newspaper that gets excerpted at the bottom of columns in *The New Yorker*. Rest assured—obscene though your paper's return on investment may be, it is never too late to find out what is really going on. With today's media, you have to read between the lines.

24·

Did Neil Armstrong Blow His Lines?

Yep. What Neil Armstrong meant to say was, "That's one small step for a man, one giant leap for mankind." But that isn't quite what he said.

The radio transmissions from the *Apollo 11* lunar module were of somewhat poor quality. If you listen to a tape of the transmissions, however, there can be little doubt as to what Armstrong did say. After setting foot on the moon, Armstrong pauses a second or two and says,

> *That's one small step for man,*
> *one giant leap for mankind.*

The omitted "a" is a small mistake but a particularly unfortunate one. "Man" without a preceding article means not one man but man in general, mankind. So Armstrong said, in effect, that's one small step for mankind and one giant leap for mankind. He managed to create a logical contradiction in the first eleven words spoken while standing on another planet.

The slip of the tongue is understandable. What's harder to understand is the way the blunder has been ignored. Despite the massive buildup given the first words on the moon's surface, no major news source seems to have mentioned the mistake, even in passing. Most newspapers and magazines at the time reported the quote accurately but without comment. *The New York Times* for July 21, 1969, noted,

> . . . Mr. Armstrong opened the landing craft's hatch, stepped slowly down the ladder and declared as he planted the first human footprint on the lunar crust:

"That's one small step for man, one giant leap for mankind."

Life magazine didn't print Armstrong's historic words, an unusual omission even in a picture magazine.

Other sources have become more charitable yet (see table). Quite a few respectable sources now give a corrected version of the line. The 1980 edition of the *Encyclopaedia Britannica* says,

At 10:56 PM EDT, July 20, 1969, Armstrong stepped from the "Eagle" onto the Moon's dusty surface with the words, "That's one small step for a man, one giant leap for mankind."

Accurate Quote but No Mention of Mistake	*"Corrected" Quote*	*No Quote*
The New York Times	Encyclopaedia Britannica	Life
The Washington Post	Encyclopedia Americana	
The Los Angeles Times	Collier's Encyclopedia	
Time	World Book Encyclopedia (entry co-written by Wernher von Braun)	
Newsweek		
Famous First Facts	People's Almanac	
	Reader's Digest	
	National Geographic (article by Armstrong, Aldrin, and Collins)	

Big Secrets' search of reference sources found only one complete account of Armstrong's words. This was in the relatively obscure *Academic American Encyclopedia,* 1980 edition (Princeton, N.J.: Aretê Publishing Company). David Dooling's entry on Neil Armstrong gives the real story:

... he planted his left foot on the lunar surface and proclaimed: "That's one small step for [a] man, one giant leap for mankind." He later said that he intended to say "a," but static on the tapes leaves this detail uncertain.

25·

Secret Radio Frequencies

Sandwiched into the gap between the AM and FM dials are hundreds of secret communications frequencies—some so secret that no one owns up to them. The usual consumer gear—AM/FM radios, TVs, CB radios—brings in only a small portion of the electromagnetic spectrum. To pick up the secret signals, you need a shortwave receiver—and you need to know the unlisted frequencies.

Allocation of radio frequencies is quirky. When you flip the TV dial from channel 6 to channel 7, you unknowingly jump over the entire FM radio band as well as such exotica as Secret Service communications and a special frequency designated for emergency use during prison riots. The U.S. government will provide information on unclassified allocations (those for the Coast Guard, Forestry Service, weather reports, etc.). But it is quiet about secret government frequencies and those of mysterious illegal broadcasters here and abroad.

Many shortwave-radio hobbyists keep track of the secret frequencies, however. Their findings appear in such publications as the *Confidential Frequency List* by Oliver P. Ferrell (Park Ridge, N.J.: Gilfer Associates, 1982 [periodically updated]), *How to Tune the Secret Shortwave Spectrum* by Harry L. Helms (Blue Ridge Summit, Pa.: TAB Books, 1981), and *The "Top Secret" Registry of U.S. Government Radio Frequencies* by Tom Kneitel (Commack, N.Y.: CRB Research, 1981 [periodically updated]). These and similar publications should be consulted for the most up-to-date listings. The selection below includes only the most noteworthy or inexplicable broadcasts.

Air Force One

Many of the in-flight phone calls from *Air Force One* are not scrambled and can be picked up by anyone with a shortwave radio. You just have to watch the newspapers for information on the President's travels and listen to the right frequencies shortly before landing or after takeoff at Andrews Air Force Base (when calls are less likely to be scrambled electronically). A presidential phone call is usually prefaced by a request for "Crown," the White House communications center.

Air Force One uses several frequencies, including those assigned to Andrews Air Force Base. Transmissions are on single, usually upper, sideband. The frequencies are nominally secret, but the frequency numbers have long since leaked out or have been discovered independently. It is suspected that wire services and TV news operations monitor them for leads. The reported frequencies (in kilohertz) are:

6,731	13,201
6,756	13,215
8,967	13,247
9,018	15,048
11,180	18,027

In addition, 162.685 MHz and 171.235 MHz are Secret Service frequencies used for *Air Force One* communications. The White House staff uses 162.850 MHz and 167.825 MHz. Secret Service channel "Oscar," 164.885 MHz, is used for the President's limousine. *Air Force Two* uses the same frequencies as *Air Force One*.

Although everyone concerned must know that outsiders may be eavesdropping, conversations are often surprisingly candid. (Shortwave-radio listeners heard the White House staff urging *Air Force Two* back to Washington after the 1981 attempt on President Reagan's life, complete with reports that then-Secretary of State Alexander Haig was "confusing everybody" with his claim of being "in control.") No law seems to forbid such eavesdropping. Ironically, it is illegal (Section 605 of the Communications Act of 1934) to reveal intercepted conversations to anyone else—that being regarded as the wireless equivalent of wiretapping. Even so, *The New York Times* has run snippets of *Air Force One* conversations.

Central Intelligence Agency

The CIA and other government agencies with clandestine operations are believed to have dozens of authorized frequencies, which may be rotated as needed to throw eavesdroppers off the track. Call letters are rarely used, and several government agencies may share the same frequencies. A further, rather thin veneer of security comes from the use of code words. Government surveillance operations use a common code: "Our friend" or "our boy" is the person being followed. "O" is his office; "R" is his residence. A "boat" is a car. Once apprehended, a suspect is a "package" and may be taken to the "kennel," the agents' headquarters. Does this fool anyone? Probably not.

Not all U.S. government broadcasts can be identified as to agency. Conversations are cryptic; letters to the Federal Communications Commission and Commerce Department bring form replies. These frequencies (in megahertz) have been identified with the CIA:

163.81
165.01
165.11
165.385
408.60

Drug Enforcement Administration

Reported frequencies are:

11,076 KHz	418.625
14,686	418.675
18,666	418.70
163.185MHz	418.725
163.535	418.75
165.235	418.775
165.285	418.80
165.29	418.825
172.00	418.875
172.05	418.90
172.20	418.925
415.60	418.95
416.05	418.975
416.20	419.00

Federal Bureau of Investigation

Reported frequencies are:

7,905 KHz	167.395
9,240	167.40
10,500	167.41
120.425 MHz (?)	167.425
149.375	167.435
163.31	167.45
163.485	167.46
163.81	167.475
163.825	167.485
163.835	167.50
163.875	167.51
163.885	167.525
163.91	167.55
163.925	167.56
163.935	167.575
163.95	167.585
163.96	167.60
163.975	167.61
163.985	167.625
164.26	167.635
164.275	167.65
164.41	167.66
164.46	167.675
165.525	167.685
166.50	167.70
167.15	167.71
167.21	167.725
167.22	167.735
167.235	167.75
167.25	167.76
167.26	167.775
167.275	167.785
167.285	167.805
167.30	167.875
167.31	167.925
167.325	167.985
167.335	168.885
167.36	406.20
167.375	406.25
167.385	406.275

406.30
406.325
406.35
406.375
406.40
406.45
408.85
408.875
408.90
408.925
408.95
408.975
409.00
409.025
409.05
409.10
409.15
409.175
409.20
409.25
411.025
411.075
412.425
412.45
412.475
412.50
412.55
412.575
413.425
413.55
413.975
414.00
414.025
414.05
414.075
414.10
414.125
414.15
414.175
414.20
414.225
414.25
414.275

414.30
414.35
414.375
414.40
414.425
414.45
414.475
414.50
414.525
414.55
414.575
415.75
417.075
417.15
417.40
417.45
417.50
417.55
419.20
419.225
419.25
419.275
419.30
419.325
419.35
419.375
419.40
419.425
419.45
419.475
419.50
419.525
419.55
419.575
467.95

Secret Service

Reported frequencies (in megahertz) are:

162.375	165.76
162.685	165.785
163.36	165.90
163.40	166.21
163.81	166.405
164.75	166.51
164.885	166.615
165.025	166.70
165.085	168.40
165.21	168.45
165.235	169.625
165.375	169.925
165.675	171.235
165.685	

Bugs

Room bugs are miniature radio stations. As such, anyone can tune them in. This rarely happens, though, because the range is limited and the frequency is known only to the person who placed the bug.

In practice, most bugs transmit by frequency modulation, on or near the standard FM broadcast band (88 to 108 MHz). There is a toy called Mr. Microphone that is, in effect, a bug shaped like a large hand-held microphone. The user speaks into the microphone, and others may hear his voice on their FM radios. Clandestine bugs work similarly but are more likely to transmit just off either end of the FM band—from 86 to 88 MHz (which infringes on a band allocated to television channels 5 and 6) or 108 to 110 MHz. In that way, the chance of accidental interception or of someone complaining to the Federal Communications Commission is less. The Watergate bug was to have transmitted at 110 MHz.

You can check for bugs using an FM radio. Turn the tuner to the extreme left side of the dial, as far as it will go, and turn the volume up. Although 88 MHz is the lowest frequency marked, most receivers have enough "overcoverage" to pick up 87 or 86

MHz. No FM stations are assigned below 88 MHz, so anything you may hear there is suspicious. Slowly move the dial to the right until you come to the first commercial FM station. Sweep over the FM band proper, and then check the overcoverage region above 108 MHz. Any bug you hear will be in your immediate neighborhood: Typical transmitters use a few milliwatts of power and have a range of a few hundred yards. If you suspect the bug is in a nearby room, have someone talk or play music while you scan.

A few bugs can be picked up only with special shortwave receivers. The frequencies from 48 to 50 MHz and 72 to 75 MHz are sometimes used. Several shortwave operators have reported conversations that seem to be from room bugs at 167.485 MHz—an FBI frequency.

Morse Code Letter Beacons

Dozens of low-power stations transmit only a letter of Morse code endlessly. No one, including government agencies and the International Telecommunications Union, admits to knowing where the signals are coming from, who is sending them, or why.

"K" (dash-dot-dash) is the most common letter. Letters are repeated every two to seven seconds, depending on the station. The stations never identify themselves. The frequency used for the broadcast shifts slowly with time, so this list is only an approximate guide:

Frequency (KHz)	Letter
4,005	K
4,466	U
5,306	D and W
5,307	F
5,795	K
5,890	K
5,920	K
6,203	P
6,770	A and N
6,800	F and K
6,806	Q
7,590	W
7,656	W

Frequency (KHz)	Letter
7,954	K
8,137	U
8,144	K
8,647	F
8,703	E
8,752	K
9,043	K
9,058	U
10,211	U
10,446	E
10,570	K
10,614	F
10,638	K
10,644	D
10,645	F
10,646	R and K
11,156	K
12,151	K
12,185	U
12,329	U
13,328	U
13,637	F
14,478	K
14,587	K
14,967	K
15,656	U
15,700	U
15,705	U
17,015	D
17,016	C
17,017	F
17,018	UE and TA
18,343	K
20,456	E
20,992	O and C

These stations broadcast mostly during the night hours of North America. They are most often picked up in North America, Australia, and the Orient. But because of the easy propagation of shortwave signals, no one is sure where they are coming from.

An analysis in the *Confidential Frequency List* holds that the signals are coming from 25- to 100-watt unattended transmitters somewhere in the South Pacific. An alternate theory places the Morse code "beacons" in Cuba. It is known that there used to be a "W" station operating at 3,584 KHz, a frequency supposedly reserved for amateur use. When American amateurs protested to the Federal Communications Commission about the interference, the FCC complained to the Cuban government. The station disappeared shortly thereafter.

Actually, all of the beacons must be presumed illegal. Short-wave stations are supposed to be registered with the International Telecommunications Union; none of those listed above are. The purpose of the stations is as unclear as their location. A single letter conveys no information. There are legitimate navigational beacon stations, which broadcast their call letters. But such stations are registered and operate on fixed frequencies from known locations. Keeping location and frequency information secret would defeat their purpose.

Maybe, then, the letter beacons are navigational stations operated for the benefit of a select few. Some think they are operated by the Soviet Union, in Cuba, for some military purpose. Still, the globe is crosshatched with legitimate navigational beacons. It is hard to see what further navigational aid the Soviets could expect to derive from their own secret network of beacons.

It has also been suggested that the beacon stations are really teletype or other data-transmission stations and that the Morse code letters are just a way of keeping the channel clear between data transmissions. A few of the stations started transmitting some sort of data—audible as a characteristic high-speed type-writerlike sound—in 1980. There are other ways of keeping a data channel open, though. Most radioteletype stations transmit the signal for a "space" (as between words) or a similar device between transmissions. (The radioteletype code is different from Morse code.)

Finally, still others think the letter transmissions are themselves some sort of coded message. Granted, the letter can't mean anything, but some wonder if the precise length of the interval between the letters means something. Or the frequency shifts may hold the message.

The number of Morse code letter stations seems to be increasing.

Numbers Stations

Well over a hundred "numbers" or "spy" stations have been reported, all rather closely following a pattern. On the typical numbers station, the announcer is—or seems to be—a woman. No one knows who the woman is or where she is broadcasting from. She speaks in Spanish, German, or Korean. Save for a few words at the beginning and end of the transmission, the message consists of random numbers, announced in groups of five, four, or, rarely, three digits. As with the Morse code stations, the numbers stations are all on unauthorized frequencies. No government or organization owns up to the broadcasts; officially, at least, the FCC claims no knowledge of them.

Many of those who have listened to the broadcasts carefully are convinced that the woman is in fact a robot. The voice has a mechanical ring, sometimes with a click between each digit. It seems to be the same sort of device used by the telephone company to give the time or forwarding phone numbers.

The exact format of the messages varies with the language and number of digits per group. With Spanish, five-digit groups, for instance, a typical message might be:

Atención 290 22 . . . *Atención* 290 22 . . . *Atención*
290 22 . . . 39876 . . . 11203 . . . 58888 . . .
30957 . . . 11219 . . . 95804 . . . 38502 . . .
21230 . . . 49801 . . . 98205 . . . 48290 . . .
81101 . . . 86038 . . . 28194 . . . 69301 . . .
72067 . . . 19473 . . . 18637 . . . 02731 . . .
33082 . . . 89063 . . . 99120 . . . *Final, final.*

Broadcasts are during the night hours of North America and seem to start shortly after the hour. After the *"final, final,"* the transmission stops. It is claimed that a given transmission is repeated a few minutes later on a slightly different frequency.

There seems to be no escaping the conclusion that the messages are a numerical code. The second number after the *"Atención"*—22 in the example—is the number of digit groups in the message. There doesn't seem to be any demonstrable significance to the first number. Some suspect it is an identifying number for the sender or, more likely, the receiver.

The four-digit transmissions in Spanish are different. A three-digit number (perhaps that of the sender or receiver) is repeated several times, followed by the digits 1 through 0 (*"uno, dos, tres, cuatro, cinco, seis, siete, ocho, nueve, cero"*) and a string of Morse-code dashes. The word *grupo* is followed by the number of four-digit groups to come and repeated once—for example, *"Grupo* 22, *grupo* 22." The message—groups of four Spanish-language numbers— follows. At the end the voice says, *"Repito grupo* 22," and the message repeats. The station goes off the air after the repeat.

Any attempt to explain these stations is complicated by numbers broadcasts in other languages. There are also broadcasts in German (they start with *"Achtung"* and terminate with *"Ende"*), Korean, and English. Occasional transmissions in Russian, French, Portuguese, and even Serbo-Croatian are reported. Sometimes a male (mechanical?) voice reads the numbers. The female robot voice doing English-language broadcasts is often described as having an Oriental or German accent. Typical of the uncertainty surrounding numbers stations are the reported English-language messages prefaced with a female voice saying "Groups disinformation" and ending with "End of disinformation." At least, it sounds like "disinformation." Perhaps the voice machine has a bad rendering of "this information."

Still other stations transmit messages consisting of letters from the phonetic alphabet (Alpha, Bravo, Charlie, etc.). Some spice their programs with music, which ranges from ethnic tunes to weird tones that may or may not conceal a message.

Reported frequencies for numbers and phonetic-alphabet stations include:

Frequency (KHz)	*Description*
3,060	Female reading numbers in Spanish
3,090	Female reading numbers in Spanish
3,365	Male reading numbers in Serbo-Croatian
4,640	Male reading numbers in Spanish
4,642	Female reading numbers in French
4,670	Female reading numbers and phonetic-alphabet letters in Spanish and English
4,740	Male reading numbers in Spanish and Portuguese; musical interlude from *Aïda*
4,770	Female reading numbers in German
4,792	Female reading numbers in Spanish

Frequency (KHz)	Description
5,020	Female reading numbers in Spanish
5,075	Female reading numbers in Spanish
5,110	Male reading numbers in Czech; Slavic musical interludes
5,812	Female reading numbers in Spanish
6,770	Female reading numbers in Spanish
6,790	Female reading numbers in Spanish
8,875	Female reading numbers in Spanish
9,040	Female reading numbers in English and Spanish
9,345	Female reading numbers in Spanish
9,450	Female reading numbers in English; musical tones
9,463	Female reading numbers in Spanish
9,950	Female reading numbers in Spanish
10,450	Female reading numbers in Korean
10,500	Female reading numbers in German
11,532	Female reading numbers in Spanish
11,545	Female reading numbers in German
11,618	Female reading numbers in German
11,635	Female reading numbers in Spanish
13,320	Male reading numbers in Russian
14,947	Female reading numbers in German
14,970	Female reading numbers in English; beep tones
23,120	Female reading numbers in German
30,050	English numbers
30,250	English numbers
30,420	English numbers
30,470	English numbers

Whatever is going on, it's a big operation. Harry L. Helms' *How to Tune the Secret Shortwave Spectrum* has a list of sixty-two stations that includes only those with a female voice reading five-digit numbers in Spanish. Much time and effort are going into the broadcasts. Some numbers stations transmit on upper sideband rather than amplitude modulation (upper sideband requires more elaborate and expensive equipment). Signals are usually strong. Because of ionospheric reflection, they can be picked up over most of the globe. This makes direction-finding difficult.

Two explanations are offered for the numbers stations. It is rumored that some of the stations are communications links in the drug traffic between the United States and Latin America. If so,

Spanish is a logical language. The numerically coded messages could tell couriers where drops will be made, how much to expect, and other minutiae that would change from day to day. Weak support for this explanation comes from some amateur direction-finding, which seems to place many of the Spanish-language stations somewhere south of the United States.

But even those who subscribe to this explanation agree that other numbers stations, probably most of them worldwide, are engaged in espionage—governmental or organizational communication with agents in the field.

Which government? The Spanish-language stations are usually heard between 7:00 P.M. and 6:00 A.M. Eastern Standard Time. The night hours are best for clandestine broadcasting, as weak signals propagate farther. So the Spanish-language broadcasts are probably coming from a time zone not far removed from Eastern Standard Time. (The EST zone includes the central Caribbean, Colombia, Ecuador, and Peru.)

On the basis of broadcast times and signal strengths, it can similarly be postulated that the German-language stations are coming from Europe or maybe Africa, and the Korean-language stations are coming from the Orient—reasonably enough.

As far as the Spanish-language stations are concerned, suspicion points to Cuba. In 1975 U.S. listeners reported muffled Radio Havana broadcasts in the background of some of the Spanish-language stations. A station at 9,920 KHz is said to have used the same theme music as Radio Havana.

But then there are American ham radio operators who swear that the Spanish-language stations must be in the United States. *How to Tune the Secret Shortwave Spectrum* tells of listeners in Ohio who reported four-digit-numbers stations coming in stronger than anything else on the dial except a 50-kilowatt broadcast-band station a few miles distant. Similar reports come from the Washington, D.C., area.

Probably the simplest of all the many possible explanations is that the Spanish-language stations are operated by Cuba for the benefit of Cuban agents in the United States. The Radio Havana broadcasts in the background would have been a mistake. The engineer was listening to Radio Havana and forgot the mike was on, or maybe Radio Havana and some of the numbers stations share facilities and the signals got mixed. The local-quality broadcasts heard in the United States could be Cuban agents reporting back to Havana. Each agent would have to have his own mechanical-voice setup.

The actual explanation may not be the simplest, though. According to Helms, some shortwave listeners believe that the four- and five-digit Spanish-language broadcasts are entirely different operations. The four-digit transmissions, at least some of which seem to originate in the United States, may be the work of the U.S. government. Only the five-digit transmissions may come from Latin America—and may be associated with local governments or U.S. foreign agents. Harry L. Helms speculates that the United States may have faked the Radio Havana background just to divert suspicion from an American espionage operation.

Any glib explanation of the numbers stations is further challenged by another incident Helms cites. An unnamed listener was receiving a five-digit-numbers broadcast in a female voice in Spanish. At the end of the transmission, the station (accidentally?) stayed on the air, and faint female voices were heard reading numbers in English and German. If the report is accurate, then the numbers stations could be the work of one worldwide operation. Choice of languages could be arbitrary. Whatever his or her native tongue, an agent need only learn ten words of, say, Korean in order to receive a numerical code in Korean.

No one willing to talk about it has broken the code or codes used for the transmissions. If the operation or operations are sophisticated enough, it may be pointless even to try. A random four- or five-digit number added to each number group before transmission will scramble the code. The numbers must be agreed upon by sender and receiver beforehand. If a different number is used for each number block and if they are not repeated, it is mathematically impossible for outsiders to crack the code.

Beeps, Screeches, and the Russian Woodpecker

There are still other inexplicable radio transmissions.

At 3,820 KHz there is a four-note electronic tune. The station never identifies itself; no one knows where the signal is coming from or why.

At 12,700 KHz there is a plaintive, twenty-one-note, flutelike melody.

At 15,507 KHz there are beeps.

The "Russian woodpecker" is a mysterious noise heard on frequencies ranging from 3,261 to 17,540 KHz. It is variously described as like a woodpecker or buzz saw. It was first heard in late 1976 or early 1977, seems to be coming from the Soviet Union, and is so powerful that it drowns out all other signals on its band. The usual hypothesis is that it is an experimental Soviet over-the-horizon radar system. Similarly, some think that 388.0 MHz—a frequency between VHF and UHF television carrier frequencies—is a resonant frequency of the human body being used in secret "death ray" experiments.

The most secret of transmissions are not even recognizable as transmissions. *Without Cloak or Dagger*, a 1974 book by former CIA agent Miles Copeland, tells of "screech" transmissions. These are tape-recorded messages speeded up or scrambled in such a way that they sound like radio interference. Only the intended recipient, with a variable-speed tape recorder or descrambler, can recover the messages.

More subtle yet is a device called the SC/16, manufactured by Transcript/International of Lincoln, Nebraska. The SC/16 is a "frequency-hopping" transmitter and receiver. Two synchronized units broadcast and receive at a frequency that changes every twelfth second. As many as twenty-four different frequencies are used, all between 145 and 166 MHz.

Any outsider tuning into this range would hear, at most, one-twelfth-second bursts of speech. The bursts are too fleeting to be recognized as speech; they sound like static.

26·

Secret Messages on Records

Two mentalities are at work here: 1960s rock fans and 1980s fundamentalist Christians. The idea of phonographically concealed messages dates from the Paul McCartney death scare of 1969. For hard-core types, the secret-message rumors never really died. Avid rock fans have auditioned every album release since the late 1960s for hidden nuances. Backward messages, barely audible messages, and messages on one stereo track only have been alleged. At the other end of the sociosensual spectrum, fundamentalist Christians have gotten into the act. TV programs such as *Praise the Lord* and *The 700 Club* have propagated rumors of a satanic plot in the recording industry, no less, in which various albums conceal "backward-masked" demonic murmurings. If *that* sounds too spacey to be taken seriously, consider that it was the fundamentalist groups who were behind House Resolution 6363, a bill introduced in the U.S. House of Representatives by Robert K. Dornan (R., Calif.) in 1982 to label all suspect records: "WARNING: THIS RECORD CONTAINS BACKWARD MASKING THAT MAKES A VERBAL STATEMENT WHICH IS AUDIBLE WHEN THIS RECORD IS PLAYED BACKWARD AND WHICH MAY BE PERCEPTIBLE AT A SUBLIMINAL LEVEL WHEN THIS RECORD IS PLAYED FORWARD." In February 1983, the Arkansas State Senate passed a similar record-labeling bill by a vote of 86 to 0.

Contributing to the quasi-occult status of these rumors is the difficulty of checking them out on home audio equipment. You pretty much have to take someone else's word for it, or dismiss the rumors out of hand.

From a technical standpoint, there are four simple ways to conceal a verbal message on a recording. The most obvious is to record the message at a very low volume. The message may then be recovered by turning the volume up while playing the record or tape. If the message is faint enough, though, noise levels of home equipment may garble it. If the accompanying music or lyrics are loud enough, or if the message itself is indistinct or electronically modified, it may be hard to hear on any equipment.

A second gimmick is to record a message on one stereo track only. Records and tapes have two independent recordings, of course, normally played simultaneously for stereo effect. On a record, each stereo track occupies one side of the V-shaped groove for the needle. On a tape, the tracks are recorded in parallel lanes of the magnetic material. The two tracks are called "right" and "left" after the stereo speakers they will play on. Otherwise, the tracks are interchangeable—the sound mixer can put anything he or she wants on each track. (High notes do not have to go on one track and low notes on the other.) A message on one track can be masked by simultaneous loud music or lyrics on the opposite track. With normal stereo balance (or mono equipment) the loud track drowns out the message track. At home, single-track messages can be recovered by adjusting the stereo balance so that only the desired track plays. Sometimes this trick also makes indistinct words clearer. Even if the words are not exclusively on one track, they may happen to be more audible on one track.

A message could be recorded at a speed different from the rest of the record. Then the record would have to be played faster or slower than usual to recover the message. Unless the message was at one of the standard speeds (say, 45 rpm on a 33⅓ rpm record), it could not be played normally on home equipment.

The fourth and most commonly alleged trick is to record a verbal message backward. Reversed speech has several unexpected features. One is that syllables are not a constant in the reversal process. A one-syllable word can have two or three syllables when played backward. Thus "number nine" in the Beatles' *Revolution 9* reverses to "Turn me on, dead man" (or something like it), a jump from three to five syllables.

There is no simple way to predict what a word or phrase will sound like reversed. Obviously, you can't just reverse the letters. The slightly less naïve approach of reversing phonetic spellings—

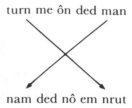

Reversed messages are difficult to recover at home. Record turntables are not built to go backward. Some have a neutral setting, in which the pickup and amplifier remain active and you can turn the record backward by hand. But hardly anyone has a steady enough hand to produce satisfactory results.

With patience, it is possible to reverse a cassette recording. Transfer the music from the original record or tape onto a blank tape cassette. Place the cassette flat on a table. Draw out the part of the tape with the suspected message and snip it off at both ends. Hold the tape segment horizontally. Rotate it 180 degrees, keeping it horizontal at all times. This turns the tape end for end. Splice the reversed tape segment back onto the two loose ends of the cassette with strong adhesive tape. Reel the tape back inside the cassette. The spliced segment will play backward on an ordinary cassette player.

Big Secrets rented a recording studio to test the secret-message rumors. New copies of the records in question were transcribed on quarter-inch master tape. Where rumor alleged that a single stereo track contained a message, right and left stereo tracks were transcribed separately. Records with alleged inaudible messages were treated similarly. To test claims of reversed messages, recordings on the master tape were edited out and spliced in backward. Twenty cuts or portions of cuts from sixteen albums were tested.

"Another One Bites the Dust"
Queen, *The Game*

Rumor: When played backward, the lyrics say, "It's fun to smoke marijuana."
Findings: There is something that sounds like "It's fun to smoke marijuana" in the reversed music. It is repeated over and over. It

might be rendered no less faithfully, however, as "sfun to scout mare wanna." This "message" is the reversal of the song title, which is repeated as a line in the song.

Let's make a distinction between engineered and phonetic reversals. When an artist records a verbal statement, reverses it by turning the tape end for end, mixes the reversed statement onto a master tape, and has records and tapes produced from the master, that is an engineered reversal. When the phonetic properties of song lyrics are such that they can be reversed to sound like something else, that is a phonetic reversal.

"It's fun to smoke marijuana" is clearly a phonetic reversal. The lyrics are perfectly plain played forward ("Another one bites the dust"), not so plain played backward ("sfun to scout mare wanna"). With an engineered reversal, the opposite should hold true: gibberish forward, clear as a bell backward. Some are prepared to believe that phonetic reversals are just as intentional as engineered reversals—that the songwriter painstakingly planned the phonetic *double-entendre*. In the absence of confirming evidence, that just doesn't wash. It's too easy to find coincidences. If, for instance, the letters of the alphabet are recited in conventional fashion (Ay, Bee, Cee, etc.) and reversed, at least five sound like English language words. D reverses to "eden," F becomes "pray," S becomes "say," V becomes "even," and Z becomes "easy." "It's fun to smoke marijuana" is likewise a coincidence.

"A Child Is Coming"
Jefferson Starship, *Blows Against the Empire*

Rumor: When played backward, "son of Satan."
Findings: Another phonetic coincidence. The repeated "It's getting better" reverses to an iffy "son of Satan," the "of" drawn out and the "Satan" strongly accented on the first syllable.

"Eldorado"
Electric Light Orchestra, *Eldorado*

Rumor: When played backward, "He is the nasty one/Christ, you're infernal/It is said we're dead men/Everyone who has the mark will live."
Findings: Coincidence. The supposed message lurks around the line "On a voyage of no return to see." Reversed, this passage be-

comes the expected syllable salad—no one hearing it cold would describe it as anything but reversed music. Only if you listen while reading along with what you're supposed to hear will you get anything. The rumored version of the message is somewhat fudged. The passage sounds more like "He's to nasty one/Christ you are, Christ, you're fernal/There wiss suh, we're dead men . . ." There is no "in" in what is taken to be "infernal." The line that is supposed to be "Everyone who has the mark will live" isn't even close, though the syllable count is about right.

"Shoo Be Doo"
The Cars, *Candy-O*

Rumor: When played backward, the word "Satan" repeated approximately eleven times.

Findings: Coincidence. The rumor refers to the reversal of the "Shoo be doo, shoo be doo, shoo be doo . . ." near the end of the song. Given the mysterious logic of reversed phonemes, these three-syllable units can be heard as a repeated two-syllable word. The word sounds a little like "Satan."

"Snowblind"
Styx, *Paradise Theater*

Rumor: According to a mimeographed list of suspect records distributed by Congressman Dornan, the words "Satan move through our voices" when played backward.

Findings: Negative. Despite repeated listenings, it was not even possible to identify the part of the reversed track that Dornan et al. are talking about.

"Stairway to Heaven"
Led Zeppelin, untitled, a.k.a. *Stairway to Heaven*

Rumor: In reverse, "I live for Satan . . . The Lord turns me off . . . There's no escaping it . . . Here's to my sweet Satan . . . There's power in Satan . . . He will give you 666."

Findings: Coincidence. If you listen very carefully to the "And it makes me wonder" lines in reverse, you'll hear something approaching "There's no escaping it." A better description is

"There's no escape do." Knock off the last syllable, and you have "There's no escape," a complete, intelligible sentence in reverse. It's there, all right, but it's not an unlikely enough coincidence to—well, make you wonder.

The "Satan" in "I live for Satan" is good and clear. The "I live for" part isn't. The other alleged lines are unremarkable. All are phonetic reversals of the entirely lucid forward lyrics and obviously just accidents.

"When Electricity Came to Arkansas"
Black Oak Arkansas, *Black Oak Arkansas* and *Ronch and Roll*

Rumor: In reverse, "Satan, Satan, Satan, Satan, Satan. He is God. He is God."
Findings: The *Black Oak Arkansas* cut was reversed. Again, pairs of reversed syllables are being freely interpreted as "Satan." "He is God" was not identifiable.

"Rain"
The Beatles, *Hey Jude*

Rumor: The unintelligible lyrics at the end are reversed.
Findings: A true engineered reversal and not really a secret. "Rain" seems to have been the first popular recording to incorporate an obviously reversed lyric. The story is that John Lennon accidentally spliced the last part of the song in backward and liked the effect. When reversed, the strange-sounding vocals at the end become intelligible as a reprise starting with the drawn-out word "sunshine."

The reversal is less apparent to the casual listener than it might be because the accompanying music is not reversed. The ending fits in smoothly with the rest of the song, the vocals suggesting a foreign language.

"Fire on High"
Electric Light Orchestra, *Face the Music*

Rumor: When played backward, "The music is reversible, but time—turn back!"
Findings: "Fire on High" is instrumental. About twenty-six sec-

onds into the music, scrambled speech is heard. It is mostly louder than the accompanying music and begins with a two-syllable unit repeated several times. The seeming speech lasts for about fourteen seconds.

Reversing the music confirms that that there is a true, engineered message. In reverse, a voice (Jeff Lynne's?) says, "The music is reversible, but time—turn back! Turn back! Turn back! Turn back!" All the words are clear and unambiguous. Anyone comparing this to the alleged reversal on ELO's "Eldorado" will have no trouble telling which is genuine.

"Goodbye Blue Sky"
Pink Floyd, *The Wall*

Rumor: In reverse, "You have just discovered the secret message."
Findings: The "secret message" is at the very end of the instrumental passage following the "Goodbye Blue Sky" vocals. It comes just before the words "What shall we do" at the start of the song that is identified as "Empty Spaces" on the record label and as "What shall we do now?" on the record sleeve. Played forward, the message is less apparent than the "Face the Music" reversal: A reasonably attentive listener might play *The Wall* through and not catch it. It suggests speech not quite close enough to be overheard. In context this is not unusual because the "Goodbye Blue Sky" instrumental passage includes "airport noises" and other sound effects. A loud climax in the music further masks the unintelligible voice.

When played backward, the voice (Roger Waters'?) plainly intones, "Congratulations, you have just discovered the secret message. Please send your answer to old Pink, care of the funny farm . . ." As the voice fades out, there may be another word— perhaps "Chalfonte" or "Chelsea"—after "funny farm."

"Heavy Metal Poisoning"
Styx, *Kilroy Was Here*

Rumor: A red sticker on the *Kilroy Was Here* album cover warns, "By order of the Majority for Musical Morality, this album contains secret backward messages . . ."
Findings: This is a case of second-generation backward-masking. Styx' *Paradise Theater* did not contain a backward message, though

a lot of people said it did. So Styx has included a sure enough backward message on *Kilroy Was Here*. It is at the very beginning of "Heavy Metal Poisoning." The reversed speech lasts about three seconds. There is no musical background. The words reverse to *"Annuit cœptis. Novus ordo seclorum."* This is the Latin motto encircling the pyramid on the back of a dollar bill. The usual translation: "God has favored our undertakings. A new order of the ages."

The cover sticker's "Majority for Musical Morality" is a fictitious Falwellesque group in the *Kilroy Was Here* video. Although the sticker suggests a plurality of "messages," only one was found.

Space between "I'm so tired" and "Blackbird"
The Beatles, untitled, a.k.a. *The White Album*

Rumor: A reversed message. At the time of the Paul-is-dead stories, the segue from "I'm so tired" to "Blackbird" was offered as evidence. It was held to contain John Lennon's voice, reversed, saying, "Paul is dead, miss him, miss him, miss him." That interpretation seems unlikely now, but there is a mysterious low muttering between the songs.

Findings: The mumbling is actually just to the "I'm so tired" side of the shiny "space" between cuts on the record. Each of the stereo tracks was recorded separately, twice, and a copy of each track was reversed. This produced four versions of the two-second passage: right forward, left forward, right reversed, and left reversed. All were equally unintelligible. It was not even apparent whether the voice is forward or reversed. Nor could John Lennon be identified as the speaker. There are nine or ten syllables. The first six (when played forward) are a two-syllable unit repeated three times. There is little or no difference between the stereo tracks. Any claimed interpretation of the sounds seems doubtful.

"Strawberry Fields Forever"
The Beatles, *Magical Mystery Tour*

Rumor: It was, of course, claimed that John Lennon says "I buried Paul" at the end. (It's forward, at the very end after the music fades to complete silence, returns, and starts to fade out again.) But Lennon told *Rolling Stone* that the words are "cranberry sauce."

Findings: They are "cranberry sauce." The "sauce"/"Paul" part is indistinct, but the first syllable sounds a lot more like "cran" than "I."

"Baby You're a Rich Man"
The Beatles, *Magical Mystery Tour*

Rumor: On one of the tracks the line "Baby you're a rich man too" is sung as "Baby you're a rich fag Jew," a dig at Brian Epstein. Or some think it's "rich fat Jew" and claim it as evidence of Beatle anti-Semitism.

Findings: Negative. The two stereo tracks are nearly identical. It's always possible to hear words as similar-sounding words, but basically, the lyrics jibe with the published version.

"Lord Have Mercy on My Soul"
Black Oak Arkansas, *Black Oak Arkansas*

Rumor: Simulated sex in the background behind Jim Dandy Mangrum's spoken prologue. Also, different voices saying different things on the two stereo tracks.

Findings: The rumors refer not to the song itself but to the prologue and the whispering behind it. The whispering starts after Mangrum's words, "God and the Devil, however you want it." Played in stereo, the whispering seems to be someone saying, "I want it, I need it, I want it, I need it . . ."

When the stereo tracks are split, it is apparent that there are two voices. The right track contains some low breathing or moaning before the whispering starts, and then a male voice repeating "I want it." The "I need it" 's begin a moment later, in a female voice on the left track. Another left-track voice repeats "Good" between the "I need it" 's in a more or less sexual 1½-second rhythm. The running-water sound at the end of the prologue is on both stereo tracks.

"Wild and Loose"
The Time, *What Time Is It?*

Rumor: Different voices on the two tracks, in the party conversation in the middle of the song.

Findings: The same assignment of genders to stereo tracks as above: male voices on the right track and female voices on the left. The main female voice switches over to the right stereo track when she talks to lead singer Morris Day.

"I Am the Walrus"
The Beatles, *Magical Mystery Tour*

Rumor: The fadeout contains several lines from *King Lear*. According to *The Beatles A to Z* by Goldie Friede, Robin Titone, and Sue Weiner (New York: Methuen, 1980), Lennon taped the lines from a BBC radio production and did not even know what play it was until years later.

Findings: Right and left stereo tracks of the ending were compared, but there was little difference. There seem to be four vocal components to the ending of "I Am the Walrus":

1. A chanted "Goo goo goo joob"—which is in the published lyrics and is taken from *Finnegans Wake*.
2. Another chant that seems to be "Oom pah, oom pah."
3. A third chant that has been identified as "Everybody's got one," beginning approximately when the "Goo goo goo joob" chant dies away.
4. The lines from *King Lear*.

Chant no. 3 makes it nearly impossible to understand the *Lear* dialog. But it fades away just before the last line from the play. For a moment at the very, very end of the record, there is only the *King Lear* recitation. If you turn the volume way up, you can hear (on both tracks) "Sit you down, Father; rest you." This is a line from Act IV, Scene iv. Once you turn to the right place in the play, it isn't too hard to hear the other lines spoken as you read along. "I Am the Walrus" contains eleven lines from *Lear*, the three characters speaking in distinct—not the Beatles'—voices:

OSWALD   Slave, thou hast slain me. Villain,
                    take my purse:
              If ever thou wilt thrive, bury my body,
              And give the letters which thou find'st
                    about me
              To Edmund, Earl of Gloucester; seek him
                    out

	Upon the English party. Oh, untimely death!
	Death!
EDGAR	I know thee well. A serviceable villain, As duteous to the vices of thy mistress As badness would desire.
GLOUCESTER	What, is he dead?
EDGAR	Sit you down, Father; rest you.

"Sheep"
Pink Floyd, *Animals*

Rumor: A Moog-modified voice recites a parody of the Twenty-third Psalm.

Findings: The part in question begins six minutes, thirty-five seconds into the cut, in an otherwise instrumental passage. In stereo you can barely hear a muffled, electronically modified voice begin, "The Lord is my shepherd/I shall not want . . ." The voice continues but is drowned out by the music and the bleating of sheep.

The two stereo tracks were split. The voice is relatively clear on the left track, all but absent from the right. Only the first two lines are directly from the Twenty-third Psalm. The rest (thirteen lines) is a passably clever parody of man/God and man/sheep relationships: "He converteth me to lamb cutlets." Pink Floyd's music publisher refused permission to print the lyrics here.

"Revolution 9"
The Beatles, untitled, a.k.a. *The White Album*

Rumor: Various reversed and/or one-track speech. The reversal of "Number nine" to "Turn me on, dead man" has pretty much been discounted as coincidence (though it is mentioned on Congressman Dornan's list).

Findings: Distinction between lyrics and any hidden message blurs on "Revolution 9." The eight-minute cut is a montage of sounds collected by John Lennon and Yoko Ono (and not by credited cowriter Paul McCartney, per *White Album* usage). It includes discordant music, radio broadcasts, sirens, applause, gunfights, sports cheers, the crackling of a fire, screams, a baby gurgling, a choir singing, and much that cannot be identified. For this investigation, "Revolution 9" was transcribed four times, twice on each stereo channel. One copy of each of the tracks was reversed. The four resulting versions were compared against each other and against the original two-channel version.

"Revolution 9" contains a lot of talking. Played in stereo, forward, the longest stretch of understandable speech is probably an announcer saying, ". . . every one of them knew that as time went by they'd get a little bit older and a little bit slower . . ."

One believable instance of reversed speech occurs: someone saying "Let me out! Let me out!" (once held to represent McCartney in his totaled Aston-Martin). Two iffy reversals occur on the backward recording of the right stereo track: "She used to be assistant" and "There were two men . . ." Neither is clear enough or long enough to be convincing. Some of the music, including the recurring theme, sounds more natural in reverse.

"Turn me on, dead man" is a typical phonetic reversal. The forward "number nine" (repeated throughout the cut) is clear; the reversal is slurred—something like "turn me on dedmun." It has been claimed that "number nine" must be pronounced with a British accent or with some careful inflection in order to reverse to "Turn me on, dead man." This seems not to be so. As an experiment, three American-accent renderings of "number nine" were reversed. All sounded about as much like "Turn me on, dead man" as the record did. Like the other phonetic reversals, "Turn me on, dead man" must be considered a coincidence.

Much of "Revolution 9" is on one stereo track only. Near the end a voice says "A fine natural imbalance . . . the Watusi . . . the twist . . . Eldorado . . . Eldorado." "A fine natural imbalance" is on the right track only, though the words that follow are in stereo. One of the longer bits of speech—"Who could tell what he was saying? His voice was low and his [unintelligible] was high and his eyes were low"—is clear on the left track, a bare whisper on the right.

There is a stereophonically concealed "secret message" on "Revolution 9." The words are on the right track. They begin about four minutes, fifty-eight seconds into the cut and run for about twenty-two seconds. They are not likely to be noticed in stereo because of the much louder left track. The sound of applause begins on the left track at about five minutes, one second into the cut. Deafening noises—the clapping, sirens, music—con-

212 | BIG SECRETS

tinue on the left track until five minutes, forty seconds. It may or may not have been Lennon's and Ono's intention to conceal the spoken passage. Given the haphazard quality of "Revolution 9," the concealment may have been accidental. To recover the passage, the left track must be switched off. The right track can then be heard to contain a sound like a stopwatch ticking, behind these words:

> So the wife called, and we better go to see a surgeon. . . . [*a scream muffles a line that sounds like* Well, what with the prices, the prices have snowballed, no wonder it's closed.] . . . So any and all, we went to see the dentist instead, who gave him a pair of teeth, which wasn't any good at all. So instead of that he joined the bloody navy and went to sea.

"A Day in the Life"
The Beatles, *Sgt. Pepper's Lonely Hearts Club Band*

Rumor: The seemingly blank grooves at the end of the record contain a note so high that only dogs can hear it, intended for Paul McCartney's dog, Martha.

Findings: Anyone who examines the record carefully will notice fifteen widely spaced grooves at the end of "A Day in the Life." They seem to contain no music. The record label lists the length of "A Day in the Life" as five minutes, three seconds. Yet, if you time it, the music seems to be over in about four and a half minutes. Certainly the "full" five minutes, three seconds are not played on the radio.

"A Day in the Life" was recorded with a forty-two-piece orchestra from the London Philharmonic. The loud climaxes were created by playing in different keys simultaneously. A synthesizer was also used.

Could a record contain a note too high-pitched for humans to hear? The sound engineer *Big Secrets* consulted didn't think so. Recording hardware is tuned to the human range of hearing and has a very poor response outside that range. The same is true for the equipment that plays back the sound. Even if the Beatles had somehow managed to record such a note, no commercial tweeter would respond to it—not if it was much more than twenty thousand cycles per second, anyway. So much for the idea of Fru-Fru being hypnotized by "A Day in the Life."

Those fifteen grooves aren't really empty, though. The end of "A Day in the Life"—starting with the final loud "daaa" and going all the way into the center of the record—was transferred to master tape and the stereo levels monitored. Initially, the final note is split evenly between stereo tracks. As it tails off, most of the note is on the right channel. The level never hits zero until the end of the record. By turning the volume up repeatedly, the final note can be heard all the way to the end.

Dogs can hear fainter sounds as well as higher sounds than humans. So at a given volume setting, a dog should be able to hear the final note longer than a human. Whether the dog hears the entire recorded note depends on the volume level and the dog.

27·

Subliminal Shots in Movies

Bona fide subliminal shots—significant action that flashes on the movie screen too quickly to be perceived consciously—are rare. The few recent examples use a different technology from the "Drink Coca-Cola" experiments in the 1950s.

The 1950s experiments used a tachistoscope, a sort of slide projector capable of flashing a still image on a screen for a split second. The movies themselves were projected separately. At a Fort Lee, New Jersey, movie theater, marketing researcher James Vicary pointed his tachistoscope at the screen and flashed two written messages during movies: "Hungry? Eat popcorn" and "Drink Coca-Cola." After trying the device for six weeks (on a total audience of about forty-five thousand people), Vicary concluded the messages were getting through. His report on the experiment claimed that sales of popcorn rose 57.8 percent and those of Coca-Cola increased 18 percent.

Vicary's experiments sparked a public outcry against subliminal advertising. What isn't so well known is that Vicary's experiments have been discredited scientifically as well as ethically. His tachistoscopic messages were on the screen for a fleeting one-three-thousandth second. Previous experiments in psychology laboratories had shown that information could be conveyed at a sub- or semiconscious level by the tachistoscope. But the shutter speeds in the laboratory experiments were usually around one-hundredth second—about thirty times slower than Vicary's device.

No scientist himself, Vicary did not design the experiment very well. Popcorn sales may have surged, but there was no control. Psychologists have since countered that the increase may have been a random fluctuation, a seasonal change of taste, or the result of expectant vendors pushing their product harder. No one else has since shown that one-three-thousandth-second messages can dictate behavior. Vicary's experiments raised an offbeat, perhaps important ethical issue, but if they caused even one person to buy popcorn or Coke, he did not demonstrate it in a way that most psychologists will accept.

So effectively did Vicary's tachistoscope blacken the name of subliminal advertising that only one instance of a high-speed ad has turned up in all the years since. This was in a Christmas-season-1973 TV commercial for a child's game, "Hūsker Dū?" Four times during the commercial, the words "Get it!" flashed for a split second. By then, the National Association of Broadcasters had long since banned subliminal material on member stations; the stations running the spot apparently were not aware of the high-speed inserts. A Federal Communications Commission warning resulted in the spots being pulled from the air in the United States.

A subliminal message need not have a commercial purpose. A very short message or shot edited into the final print of a movie will appear every time the movie is shown; no special equipment is needed.

Such tinkering is quantized. The briefest image possible is one that occupies a single frame of the film. A message or shot can last for one frame, two frames, three frames, but never less than a whole frame. Movies are projected at a rate of twenty-four frames a second. So each frame is on the screen for one-twenty-fourth second—actually, a hair less than that because the screen flickers to black for an instant while the next frame shifts into place.

A blink of an eye lasts about one-tenth second—long enough to blot out a one- or two-frame insert for a given viewer. But even a single-frame shot lasts several times longer than typical (one-hundredth-second) tachistoscopic stimuli of psych labs. How noticeable a shot is depends on the surrounding cinematography. Projected in a darkened theater, a single all-white frame surrounded by an opaque leader is visible as a flash on the screen. Of course, in a normal movie, the illusion of motion demands that single frames not be consciously perceptible.

Expectations influence perception. Movie projectionists have no trouble spotting the reel-change indicators (rough circles scratched into the upper right corner of a dozen or so consecutive frames). Yet the average viewer may sit through a two-hour movie without consciously perceiving the markings. Depending on the filmmaker's intentions and ingenuity, a shot may linger on the screen for some time and still be missed by those who don't know exactly what to look for. The subliminal grades into the merely inconspicuous.

Some avant-garde filmmakers have toyed with single-frame shots. Robert Breer's *Images by Images I* (1954) consists entirely of single-frame images. In a sense, the whole film is "subliminal" material. The eye adjusts to the visual anarchy enough to pick out many individual images, though.

Tony Conrad's *The Flicker* (1966) alternates all-black and all-white frames for an effect aptly described by the title. (The film is claimed to be dangerous for epileptics.)

Narrative films with significant hidden content are few and far between. The short list below does not include one sometime candidate, *The Texas Chainsaw Massacre* (New Line Cinema, 1974). Director/cowriter Tobe Hooper raised eyebrows in a 1977 *New Times* interview by acknowledging subliminal techniques in the film. Hooper denied any one-frame shots, however. If there is hidden content in *Chainsaw,* no one seems to have identified it.

My World Dies Screaming, retitled Terror in the Haunted House
Precon Process and Equipment Corporation, c. 1958

Psychologist Robert Corrigan and engineer Hal C. Becker founded the Precon Process and Equipment Corporation in New Orleans to exploit a tachistoscopic device of their invention, the "Precon." In the late 1950s, they produced two ultralow budget horror films "in Psychorama." The first, *My World Dies Screaming,* was shown in the United States and (as *Terror in the Haunted House*) Great Britain. Apparently it is no longer in release. According to descriptions, there are four embedded images. A tachistoscopic skull is supposed to evoke death; a pair of beating hearts suggests love; a snake projects hate; the word "BLOOD" reinforces fear. There is no indication that the film was any more emotionally riveting because of these devices.

A Date with Death
Precon Process and Equipment Corporation, c. 1959

Corrigan and Becker's other film.

The Exorcist
Warner Brothers, 1973

The Exorcist is apparently the only major-studio release to use sub-liminal inserts. The plot follows a young girl, Regan, who is possessed by the devil. A priest, Father Karras, is called in to exorcise the demon. Of the many special effects used by director William Friedkin, one is very brief shots of a ghoulish face. In a dream, Karras sees his mother coming out of a subway—and the face flashes on the screen. Later, Karras tries to kill Regan, and the face shot is repeated.

If you examine a print of the film, you find that the shots last two frames. The face is on the screen for one-twelfth second—rather on the longish side of subliminal. No one who knows about the face should have much trouble getting a glimpse of it. But nearly everyone who did not know about the face when they saw the movie does not remember seeing it.

The spliced-in frames show a ghostly white face looking something like Father Karras (perhaps it is Karras with different makeup). The mouth and eyes are outlined in red. The face wears a white shroud. Later in the film, when Karras becomes possessed, his face turns pale, much like the subliminal face.

It has also been claimed that the word "PIG" appears subliminally. The word appears as a graffito near the stairs behind the house. It is never on the screen for more than a moment.

It is a moot point whether the subliminal material makes the film any scarier. Neither the two-frame face nor the graffito "PIG" is particularly gruesome compared to the rest of the film. If they have any effect at all, it can only be to create a sense of apprehension. They may not even do that.

Dark Star
Jack H. Harris, 1974

Dark Star, John Carpenter's first film, has a cult following on late-night television. It is a science-fiction comedy shot for sixty thousand dollars with a group of Carpenter's fellow University of Southern California students. The script is bright, the special effects cheesy: One "space suit" was reportedly made from a cookie tin, a vacuum-cleaner hose, and styrofoam packing material from a typewriter case. The *Dark Star* is a spaceship that locates "unstable" worlds and destroys them. The lately psychotic crew is captained by a dead but still conscious commander in the ship's deep freeze. One of the ship's cache of introspective bombs must be talked out of premature explosion. The film's brief hidden message is flashed momentarily on a computer panel: "FUCK YOU HARRIS."

Who is Harris? He is Jack H. Harris, the film's producer and distributor. Best known for *The Blob* and *The Eyes of Laura Mars*, Harris backed *Dark Star* after Carpenter and friends' self-funding (some six thousand dollars) ran out. In its first celluloid incarnation, *Dark Star* ran for forty-five minutes on sixteen-millimeter stock. Harris' money bankrolled another thirty-eight minutes' worth of footage and the transfer to thirty-five-millimeter stock necessary for commercial release. Be that as it may, a rift developed between Carpenter and Harris. Carpenter and cowriter Dan O'Bannon were perfectionists; Harris was a corner-cutter. At one point Carpenter and O'Bannon allegedly sabotaged the sound track so that Harris would have to move the work from a discount film dubber to Metro-Goldwyn-Mayer.

Dark Star had limited distribution in its 1974 release. It was rereleased after *Star Wars* and has been popular in revival since. Local TV stations presumably are not aware of the fleeting obscenity, but the film is often heavily edited for television.

28·

Is Walt Disney Frozen?

Lots of people think that Walt Disney is frozen. Some say his icy remains are in a special chamber beneath the Pirates of the Caribbean exhibit at Disneyland. Some think his body is in a Salt Lake City deep freeze. It is known that there is a secret apartment in one of the spires of the Cinderella Castle at the Orlando Disney World, built for Disney and family but (they say) never occupied. Is the late animator awaiting reanimation? The story gets a lot of play at Holmby Hills cocktail parties and elsewhere. The Disney family never has said what it did with Walt's body. And as Disney's studio told the press after his death, "The entire corporation is carrying on exactly as if Walt were here."

The rumor of Disney's "cryonic suspension" has been floating around the Disney organization, cryonics groups, and much of the nation since the cartoonist's 1966 death. No one seems to know where or how the story started. Anthony Haden-Guest mentioned it in a 1973 book, *The Paradise Program* (New York: William Morrow). It has turned up in the pages of *Playboy*. Cryonics popularizer Robert C. W. Ettinger has acknowledged the rumor but discounts it. One version of the tale, it should be noted, contends that Disney was frozen but his family had second thoughts and thawed him out again. Poor Walt—first everyone said he was a pothead and now this.

The premise of cryonics is that bodies may be preserved at or before death by freezing and kept in a changeless frozen state indefinitely. It is postulated that the supertechnology of a future age will be able to revive the frozen bodies and cure them of disease or injury now untreatable. The cryonics movement generated popular interest after the publication of *The Prospect of Immortality* by Robert C. W. Ettinger, a Michigan college instructor, in 1964 (Garden City, N.Y.: Doubleday). Since then at least thirty-two people have been frozen.

No celebrities have been frozen. There are stories that Omar Bradley and Dwight Eisenhower considered it, but they most certainly were not frozen. Among living notables, sixties guru Timothy Leary and Columbia University physicist Gerald Feinberg are said to have expressed interest. TV comedy writer Dick Clair (half of the team that includes wife Jenna McMahon) plans to be suspended. But nearly all the people frozen so far are middle-class Americans—housewives, a few kids, salesmen, teachers. That's it, unless there is something to the Disney rumors.

Disney had opportunity to hear about cryonics. Ettinger's theories received widespread attention in the two years before Disney's death. (Ettinger made a tour of talk shows, getting into a televised argument with Buddy Hackett when Hackett made jokes about cryonics. Ettinger didn't see what was so funny.) If Disney was frozen, he would have been the first, barring any other clandestine freezings. Disney died just a month before Dr. James Bedford, a Glendale, California, psychology professor who received publicity as "the first frozen man."

An Old Polo Injury

There was no news coverage of Disney's funeral. Likewise, even as Disney's health failed in late 1966, he kept tight rein on media coverage of his condition.

On November 2, 1966, Disney was admitted to St. Joseph's Hospital, just across the street from his Burbank studios. Studio officials, who handled all of Disney's personal publicity, said he was to be treated for an old neck injury received while playing polo.

While in the hospital, surgeons removed part of Disney's left lung on November 21. A tumor had been found, according to a press release, but the studio refused to say whether it had been malignant. Disney was released. He was readmitted on December 5. This time he was said to be undergoing a routine postoperative checkup. Disney remained in the hospital until his death.

Hospital sources said that Disney died at nine thirty-five on the morning of December 15. Cause of death was not announced: A press release said only that Disney had suffered "acute circulatory collapse." In other words, his heart suddenly stopped beating—which, presumably, is how they decided he was dead in the first place.

On the evening of December 16, the studio unexpectedly announced that funeral services had already been held. "The services were a closely guarded family secret," observed the *Los Angeles Times*, "and were announced only after they had been concluded." The ceremony was conducted at the Little Church of the Flowers in Forest Lawn Memorial Park, Glendale. The *Los Angeles Times* reported that studio and Forest Lawn officials refused to reveal any further details of the service, including the disposition of the body. "Mr. Disney's wishes were very specific and had been spelled out in great detail," the *Times* quoted a Forest Lawn spokesman.

If you want to believe the cryonics rumor, there is further circumstantial evidence. Disney had a long preoccupation with death.

In *The Paradise Program*, Anthony Haden-Guest notes Disney's "sombre sense of death" and "occasional touch of the horrors," telling of a gruesome seven-minute Mickey Mouse cartoon made in 1933, two years after Disney's nervous collapse. In it, a mad scientist tries to cut off Pluto's head and put it on a chicken. The film was withdrawn from the Rank film library in 1970.

In *The Story of Walt Disney*, a 1957 biography, daughter Diane Disney Miller and Pete Martin write:

> It may have been while he was undergoing the nervous wear and tear which led to his crack-up that he became concerned with the inevitability of death. Mother [Mrs. Lillian Disney] says that she first noticed his brooding about that after a party twenty years ago when a fortuneteller told him that he would die when he was thirty-five.
>
> But my mother's sister, Aunt Hazel, says he still worried about that prophecy even after he passed his thirty-fifth year. Whenever father gets depressed, he discusses his impending demise. He never goes to a funeral if he can help it. If he has to go to one it plunges him into a reverie which lasts for hours after he's home. At such times he says, "When I'm dead I don't want a funeral. I want people to remember me alive."

Cryonics is expensive. Ettinger estimated the cost of a cryonics suspension in the mid-1960s as eighty-five hundred dollars minimum. Currently Trans Time, a Berkeley, California, cryonics organization, sets sixty thousand dollars as rock bottom for undertaking and for setting up a fund to pay for the costs of suspension in perpetuity. Disney's estate was said to be worth many millions of dollars. He did set up three trust funds and a foundation, the details of which were not released. (One of the trust funds endows the California Institute of the Arts, a Valencia, California, creative arts college since nicknamed Walt's Tomb or the Magic Mausoleum.)

Add to that the fact that Disney was the ultimate technology freak. Tomorrowland, monorails, Space Mountain, EPCOT . . . it isn't hard to believe that he might have been intrigued with cryonics.

A Search for Disney's Grave

What, then, happened to the body?

Regardless of the family's wishes, a death certificate must be filed, and certain information must be provided on it. Disney's death certificate is available—to anyone—from the Los Angeles County registrar-recorder's office.

It contains information that did not appear in any newspaper account of the death. The attending physician, Dr. Bert H. Cotton, listed the cause of death as "cardiac arrest" due to "bronchogenic ca lt lung." The latter is shorthand for bronchogenic *carcinoma, left* lung—that is, a cancer arising in the air passages of the left lung. Three months is given as the approximate interval between onset and death. Disney probably knew about the cancer well before the "polo injury" trip to the hospital.

The cause-of-death information on the certificate is said to have been determined from an operation November 7. This was prior to the operation disclosed to the press, which took place on November 21. The November 21 operation seems to have been his last.

The certificate says that Disney's body was cremated at Forest Lawn, Glendale, on December 17, 1966. No autopsy was performed, but there is an embalmer's signature—"Dean Fluss"— indicating that the body was embalmed.

The embalmer's name and license number check out. Fluss was indeed a real embalmer working at Forest Lawn and not a fake identity cooked up to cover a cryonics trail. When contacted, Fluss's wife said she had never heard of the cryonics rumor.

The death certificate does not say what was done with the remains. Generally speaking, though, the Forest Lawn mortuary is for those who will be interred at Forest Lawn.

The Forest Lawn management is circumspect with a vengeance. Excavated earth from fresh graves is covered with Astroturf, lest anyone be reminded that the deceased are buried in ordinary dirt. No photographs taken at Forest Lawn, including several taken for this chapter, are ever allowed to be published. The information office usually refuses to say where famous people are buried. But if you ask for the location of the marker for Walter Elias Disney, the attendant first looks in the records and then says that they are not allowed to give out that information—thus confirming that Disney *is* at Forest Lawn after all.

Big Secrets located Disney's gravesite. Much like Disneyland, Forest Lawn is divided into thematic sections: Slumberland, Vale of Memory, Babyland, etc. Disney's gravesite is in an area known as the Court of Freedom. This is on the eastern extremity of the park, about as far from the entrance as possible.

At the eastern end of the Court of Freedom is a majestic marble building, the Freedom Mausoleum. It contains the remains of several celebrities (Gracie Allen, Francis X. Bushman, Gummo Mark, Larry of the Three Stooges). Disney's site is not inside the mausoleum but in a small private garden snug against the front wall and far to the left of the mausoleum's main entrance. It is in the corner formed where the front of the mausoleum abuts a gray brick wall. The garden is enclosed with a low wall and gate (not locked). Inside is a marble bench, azalea and holly plantings, and a green-patinaed statue of a small girl. A metal plaque on the brick wall contains spaces for eight names. Disney's name is in the top space. Robert B. Brown, a son-in-law, is listed third.

The only thing even slightly unusual about the site is the wall on which the plaque rests or, more exactly, what's behind it. The wall continues far beyond the Disney family's small garden. The wall has only a few doors, normally kept locked. Behind the wall is an enclosed area not accessible from any side.

A secret cryonics vault? No. A workman left one of the wall

doors open on the day of this investigation. The hidden space is a storage area, with tools and nursery stock. The only thing on the part of the wall opposite from the Disney marker is a paper-towel dispenser for workers. Walt Disney was cremated, if in secrecy, and has a perfectly ordinary gravesite.

It is easy to guess how the cryonics rumor may have gotten started. Disney had a neurotic fear of death. He wanted people to remember him alive. So he arranged beforehand for there to be no press coverage of his funeral. He specified that the public never be told the location of his grave. The utter secrecy was unusual; it stuck in people's minds. A few weeks later and purely by coincidence, the first cryonics suspension took place. Somebody made the connection and wondered if Disney had been frozen too.

Index